S. M. B

D0899934

# INK ON MY FINGERS

# INK ON MY FINGERS

## J. H. CRANSTON

**Author of**

*Etienne Brûlé: Immortal Scoundrel*

The Ryerson Press — Toronto

*Published May, 1953*

## *Publisher's Note*

The author of this book was taken before his
memoirs were ready for the press. Fortunately
his son, William H. Cranston, his successor as
editor and publisher of *The Midland Free Press
Herald,* had been familiar with the work as it
progressed through first and second drafts, and
so could give the manuscript final editing for
the press, revise proofs, and in all ways see the
book through as his father would have done. It
is a great pleasure for us to make this acknowledgment of a most helpful collaboration.

PRINTED AND BOUND IN CANADA
BY THE RYERSON PRESS, TORONTO

*To My Wife*
EVA WILKINS CRANSTON
*and My Sons*
BILL *and* TOM

# FOREWORD

*Bodies and Souls*

MAY I INTRODUCE you to some of the bodies in my morgue.

The morgue is one of the most important departments of any newspaper. In it are carefully stored away all the clippings, photographs, and other material relative to the important people and events of the international, national, and local scene.

Indeed the morgue is the newspaper's memory. And it is a much more cheerful place than its name indicates for its contents deal more with the living than the dead.

Here, from the drawers of memory then are stories of the men and women with whom I have worked in over half a century of Canadian journalism. Their bodies were, or still are, inhabited by exceedingly lively spirits. You will already know most of them by name and reputation. It is merely my hope that, through this book, you may know them better.

In my seventy-two years I have had perhaps a unique opportunity to serve and observe my fellow men—as paper boy, clerk in my father's bookstore, printer's devil, reporter on small city dailies, editor of Canada's largest week-end journal, and more latterly as publisher of a town weekly newspaper.

Personally I would have been quite satisfied to leave it at that. The ink was running thin in my veins. But Lorne Pierce, editor of The Ryerson Press, had other ideas. He was certain that there was still one more story to tell. So I have set down some of the things which have happened since first I learned to set type, run presses, and clean up messes.

I regret that the earlier days of my life and my twenty-nine years on the *Toronto Star* have taken up so much space and that so little has been left for the most important and soul satisfying work that I

did as editor and publisher of a town weekly newspaper. In a great
city an editor seldom gets to know the people he serves. There are
too many of them and their interests are too varied. But in the smaller
communities, the editor works shoulder to shoulder with men and
women he knows, respects, and admires. He shares with them a
common purpose, the welfare of their town and countryside. The
weekly editor has the prize job in journalism.

But even there, few of us who write or publish for a living realize
just how potent for good or ill is the work we do.

Some years ago, Ilya Ehrenburg pointed out that writers were,
and still are, the conscience of their people.

Much is given to us. Much is expected of us. We must speak
against those things which are wrong: we must champion the good:
and we are equally responsible for our silences, for our failure to
expose evil and uphold the right.

I have tried in these pages to deal both justly and kindly with
those of whom I write, conscious always that, because of my limitation
of knowledge, neither full justice nor full charity has been accorded.
Yet I say sincerely that I have tried, remembering now, as I have
through the years, that no man can escape responsibility for every
word he writes and that those who report and edit are, in very truth,
dealers in men's souls.

*Midland, Ontario*
*December, 1952.*

# CONTENTS

# 1 ⋘

## *The Birth of a Notion*

A SIXTEEN-YEAR-OLD printer's devil, with smudged face, dirty hands and grimy overalls, crawled on his hands and knees under the dripping Campbell press in the plant of the old *Galt Reformer.*

With a handful of cotton waste, he began to wipe pools of oil from the galvanized iron floor.

I was that devil.

There was ink on my fingers in 1896, and there has been ever since.

Many years before, however, heredity had marked me for journalism. As I look back over close to three-quarters of a century, I cannot see how I could have done anything else.

I was the eldest of six vigorous sons of James Kersel Cranston and his wife, Eva McLean. Mother was the daughter of Robert McLean, a Scot from Inverness, secretary of Toronto's Reform Association, and an ardent politician. Every election saw him heartbroken because of the perfidy of Tory Toronto.

Father, the son of Alexander Cranston, Scottish pioneer from Roxboroughshire, was a born propagandist. To a somewhat shy and retiring son, his stream of letters in the local press were a perpetual embarrassment. But they must have carried some weight in adult circles for he was twice elected to serve as alderman on the town council.

Moreover, from time to time, father published for private distribution pamphlets on religious as well as secular subjects. He was the leader of a group of seven earnest Christians who were expelled as heretics from the Presbyterian Church because they persisted in preaching on street corners and in their homes doctrines which were deemed contrary to the creeds of the Church. James Cranston was an individual who not only held strongly and sincerely to his convictions but felt he had a responsibility to make them known to all who would read or listen.

I was brought up in the biggest bookstore in Galt, Ontario, then a town of about 6,500. My father was not a bookish man but he had certain literary principles. He sold books, magazines and newspapers as grocers sell oranges and bananas. He would sell nothing that was even tainted, let alone rotten. If he became suspicious of a book's contents, he would take it off the shelves and burn it. Playing cards he refused to sell because they might be used for gambling.

But his store carried a plentiful supply of G. A. Henty's sugar-coated British history yarns, *Robinson Crusoe, The Swiss Family Robinson,* Scott's *Waverley* novels, Cooper's *Leatherstocking Tales,* the *Boys' Own Annual* and *Chums.* There was a taste of Dickens, and of Mark Twain and Artemus Ward for humour. With such easy access to books, I early became an omnivorous reader, borrowing three or four volumes from father's shelves every week-end and returning them Monday morning. Artemus Ward was a special favourite of mine and much of his lecture on the Mormons I could repeat by heart.

The Mechanics' Institute, as the municipal Galt library was then called, also had me as a steady customer, but I did not neglect the newspapers. I read the Toronto *Globe* first—I had a *Globe* paper route—and then, if I had time, the *Mail,* the *Empire,* and the *World.* Each day after lunch I cycled down town to the local newspaper offices to get the latest sporting, political, and other news before going back to school.

But the first vague idea that I might some day become a reporter came not from any love of literature but from a juvenile effort to exterminate "Demon Rum." I inherited a deep hatred of him and of all his works from my grandfather Robert McLean, a then rare combination of Highland Scot and teetotaler who had won fame by staging the first whiskeyless barn raising in Ontario's Oxford County. My father was also an ardent temperance man.

The barroom was in ill repute and, at the advanced age of fourteen, prohibition seemed to me the only practical solution. So I despatched a letter to Wilfrid Laurier, newly chosen chief of the Liberal party at Ottawa, expressing the hope that, when he came to power, the liquor traffic would be wiped out.

I had another worry at the time. The name of James Livingstone, our Liberal member for South Waterloo riding in which Galt was located, seldom if ever appeared in the House of Commons news reports. Could a member of parliament who made no speeches be worth his salt? I included this second problem in the same letter in the secret hope that Laurier would take Livingstone to task.

On May 9, 1895, in a two-page, hand-written epistle, the federal Liberal leader replied:

My dear young friend:

I received and read with great interest your favour of the 6th inst. You will perhaps not be altogether surprised if I tell you that, while I duly appreciate the knowledge which you already possess of the most important questions which now affect our common country, and the interest you take in them, I do not altogether agree with some of the views which you express, and probably when you have reached my age, you will have modified them considerably.

You have all the enthusiasm of your age. It is an advantage which is perhaps of greater value than the experience which must follow, and which will expose it to rude shakings.

It is my intention to visit Galt and vicinity during the coming summer, and if you will then do me the pleasure of calling on me and of recalling this correspondence, we will then discuss the different questions alluded to in your letter.

The member for South Waterloo, Mr. Livingstone, is not very often heard in debate, but the House of Commons, which is composed of 215 members, would be absolutely intolerable if all the members thereof were debaters. Every man has his usefulness, and a man, who, like Mr. Livingstone, is endowed with sound common sense and good character, is a credit to his party and the House of Commons.

Believe me, my dear young friend,

Yours very sincerely,

Wilfrid Laurier.

When Laurier came to Galt I donned my best Sunday suit and called at the home of the Hon. James Young, where he was being entertained. I was ushered into the library where a number of Liberal politicians, including Registrar George Pattullo, of Woodstock, were waiting the dinner call. Pattullo, sensing my nervousness, spoke kindly. "Boy," he asked, "are you a newspaper reporter?"

"No, sir," I stammered. But the question startled me. It was the birth of a notion, a chance inquiry which, more than anything else I can recall, pointed the path of my future.

A moment later I was ushered into the great man's presence. He was then comparatively young and slight. Of above average height, he was handsome, though somewhat pale and ascetic.

Laurier greeted me warmly and asked that I be seated directly opposite him at dinner. I ate little, being much too busy feasting my eyes. The meal over, I took my leave and hurried at top speed to the town hall where a politician, who had been at the Young home, took me in tow and seated me for the public meeting on the platform with the bigwigs. It was a day which will never fade in my memory.

In 1908, as the parliamentary correspondent at Ottawa of the Toronto *Star,* I went one day to the Prime Minister's office and presented to the then Sir Wilfrid Laurier the letter he had written thirteen years before to a precocious school boy.

He read it carefully, looked up, smiled, and asked: "Well, was I right?" I had to confess that he was.

After my encounter with Laurier, I could hardly wait to write all about it to my Grandfather McLean. I was sure he would be greatly pleased since he was a strong Liberal.

His reply all but broke my heart. Grandpa had once been a schoolteacher, and had never recovered from the idea that it was his duty to correct and admonish the young, particularly his grandchildren. He wrote:

My dear Grandson:

I received your long and very interesting letter describing your interview with Mr. Laurier. The letter upon the whole is very creditable to you. The writing is good and the composition for a beginner is creditable.

Your adjectives are sometimes misplaced; for instance, you say the demonstration was a "tremendous success." "Great success" would be more appropriate. *Demonstration* should not begin with a capital "D."

Then you say "I went up to Young's." You should say *Mr. Young's.* I do not blame you for accepting the pressing invitation of Mrs. Young and Miss McNaught to have some dessert. You have only one "s" in desert.

You said you were "awfully afraid" you were not eating the grapes in a proper manner. "Awfully" is not the proper word. It should be "greatly afraid." "Awfully uncomfortable" would read better if you said "very uncomfortable."

The sentence in which you said you made a "new record" in going from Mr. Young's to the hall is well conceived and reads well.

You seem to have a liking for the word "awful." You speak of an "awful" crush. *Great* crush would be more appropriate.

You say that you finally managed to get a seat on the platform. Well, I must say, to use a slang expression, that you had a good deal of cheek. I did not notice your name in the papers as occupying a seat on the platform.

Speaking of the cheering that took place when Mr. Laurier entered the hall, and while Mr. Moore was speaking, you say that "I think that he thought, etc." This would be better expressed by saying "I suppose he thought" or "he was under the impression that he, (Mr. Moore), was the object of the cheers."

You say *"Gibson and Flatt."* You should have said Messrs. Gibson and Flatt. "Connelly" is not spelled "Conoly." You wrote the word "which" thus: "wh-ich," turning from one line to the next. A syllable should not be divided. This is the worst mistake in your letter.

Speaking of Mr. Laurier you say *"He beats everything I ever heard as a speaker."* Now Herbie, Mr. Laurier is not a thing, but a person. You should have said that he "beat every *person* you ever heard," and more eloquently you might have said that he was "the most eloquent and forceful speaker you ever heard."

Upon the whole, however, I congratulate you on the excellence of your second attempt at letter writing. I will be happy to hear from you at any time when you have occasion for letting me know of anything of importance which may occur in Galt.

I am, dear Herbie,

Your affectionate grandfather,

Robert McLean

Toronto, 28th October, 1895.

I had not only taken my first step toward reporting; I had also received from an editor my first rejection slip.

# 2 ⫷⫷⫷

## *Spit Bombing the Devil*

DESPITE Grandpa McLean, the writing bug had bitten me, and bitten me hard.

At Galt Collegiate I started to write school news for the two town papers and asked no pay. To see my copy in print was reward enough.

But in September, 1896, when I joined the staff of the weekly Galt *Reformer,* it was as a printer's devil. The wages were $2 weekly and the hours, 7 a.m. to 6 p.m., six days a week.

Andrew Laidlaw, the *Reformer's* publisher, sent me to the back shop and forgot me. He was much more interested in his prize kennels than in his employees, and no one in Galt was much surprised when the business ultimately also went to the dogs.

Printers' devils in my day lived as close to hell as their fellow printers could contrive. My duties included lifting the heavy newspaper forms from the press to the sink where, with scrubbing brush and diluted lye, I scoured off the ink. I washed the press rollers with kerosene, wiped up the presses, picked up the waste paper, and swept the floors. Any "spare" time was spent learning "the case," which meant memorizing the arrangement of type in the wooden trays in which it was stored, compartment by compartment, for hand setting.

I did not mind the dirt—though my mother must have often wished I had chosen a cleaner trade—but what I did object to was being made a target for the staff's expert chewers. One in particular could propel a bomb of juicy tobacco with pin point precision at a range of over twelve feet. So I left the *Reformer* and tried my luck with the Galt *Reporter,* the Tory daily down the street.

Here the chaps were more kindly, but they also liked their fun. On the top floor of the *Reporter* building lived Professor Baker, a

6

crabbed, hot-headed, old music teacher. The newest apprentice was invariably sent upstairs on press day to deliver "his paper" to the professor. When the boy knocked and tendered the paper a volcano erupted. The air was blue with curses. If he was not able to get away quickly, the lad was kicked down the stairs where the pranksters waited to break his fall. Somehow, however, I sensed danger, escaped, and left my fellow printers somewhat disappointed.

The first part of my day was usually spent in the composing and press rooms. Soon I was able to set the headings for the four page paper. I practised on the Rogers Typograph, made in Walkerville, Ontario, one of the first typesetting machines used in smaller Ontario towns and cities. Much lighter than the modern linotype, its characters were stamped on matrices fifteen inches or more in length, which hung in a semi-circle at the top of the machine and slid down wires into position in the casting box when the proper keys were touched. Also included in my work was the setting of "ads," auction sale bills, and funeral cards.

Hardest and most nerve-wracking job, however, was running the big Wharfedale newspaper press. When the wheels started, the noise it made, and the vibrations it caused, could be heard and felt over the entire building. It literally pounded out the papers, each revolution of the cylinder being completed with a loud knock. Not content with that, the press had a mania for pulling out type. Old John Bittman, the foreman, hovered over her like an agitated hen watching a brood of chicks. Whenever type threatened to break loose, John would pound in a sharp wooden sliver to hold it in place. Feeding 1,500 papers daily through that thundering monster was an ordeal.

Business office duties occupied part of my afternoons. I ran errands, collected advertising and job printing accounts, and often canvassed the countryside on my bicycle for overdue subscription payments and renewals.

Before a month passed, however, I was sent for three days to Berlin (now Kitchener) to cover the county assizes, and at last was on my way to becoming a reporter.

# 3 ⫷⫷⫷

## *The Thin Man*

IN MY DAY three men owned and operated the Galt *Reporter*—James
Peter Jaffray, grandson of one of the paper's founders; Thomas H.
Sears, founder of the Preston *Progress* and Hespeler *Herald* which he
sold to move to Galt; and Charlie Knowles, a quiet and retiring Galt
job printer who, after a year as a publisher, returned to his former
business.

J. P. Jaffray was a unique figure in Canadian journalism. Had
fate placed him in the editorial chair of a large daily, he would have
won national renown. Instead he chose to live in a comparatively
small community, and left an enduring mark on his native town.

In appearance alone he was unforgettable. He was thin from
head to toe. Even the straggly whiskers which covered his cheeks and
chin failed to give width to a long and narrow head. Small, beady
eyes were deeply inset behind thick glasses. Fingers, long and bony,
showed the hands of an artist.

Jaffray was highly nervous and short in the grain. The *Reporter*
once advertised for a man to cover the Preston and Hespeler beat.
Tom Arntfield, a tall, ungainly German lad, whose doctor had, for
health reasons, ordered him out of the Forbes Woollen Mills at
Hespeler, applied for the job. He had little education and absolutely
no experience but, because he was the only applicant, business manager Arthur Donaldson hired him, and sent him upstairs to "J. P." for
instructions.

Tom was nervous. "My name," he stammered after waiting some
time for Jaffray to look up, "is Arntfield. I've just been hired to write
your Preston and Hespeler news. Mr. Donaldson said you would tell
me what to do."

Jaffray, deep in one of his blistering editorials, raised his eyes, surveyed his new hand, and, glowering over his spectacles, exclaimed vehemently: "Get church news, get lodge news, get any damn news, and get to hell out of here!"

That constituted the beginning and the end of Arntfield's newspaper training. He was with the *Reporter* more than a score of years until he headed north and struck it rich. He never learned to write legibly or spell correctly, but he knew everybody and he knew news. His fame is now perpetuated in the Arntfield mine and the Northern Ontario town of the same name.

Born in Galt, in 1854, Jaffray began his newspaper career at the age of twelve on the *Weekly Reporter,* then published by his three uncles, Richard, Robert, and Henry Jaffray. After two years in the back shop, he took up telegraphy and, by the time he was eighteen, was in charge of the Dominion Telegraph Company's office at the Ontario Parliament buildings in Toronto. He went from there to a similar post at the House of Commons in Ottawa but found that the long hours seriously curtailed his sporting activities. So he returned to journalism and, with his brother Robert, founded the Norwich, Ontario, *Gazette.* Later, joined by a third brother, the Jaffrays purchased the Brantford *Union,* turned it into a daily, and ran it for three years before selling and moving to the United States. In Chicago they founded the *Canadian American,* a weekly serving Canadian-born immigrants to the United States. In 1896, however, J. P. Jaffray returned to the Galt *Reporter* and converted it from weekly to daily publication.

Galt then, like many other Ontario towns, was shabby. Long grass and weeds grew in the streets, and few citizens cared how they kept their lawns and gardens. Within six weeks after his return, "J. P." told the Scottish folk, who formed the majority of Galt's residents, to clean up, take down their high board fences, trim their grass, and establish some parks. They did not like it and called him a "Yankee upstart."

"J. P." kept on. People began to take notice. Lawns were mowed and gardens planted. Fences and weeds disappeared. Land was set aside for new parks. Today Galt is one of the most beautiful small cities on the continent. Those who remember give credit to Jaffray.

I have preserved only one sample of Jaffray's editorial style and I doubt if it is a fair one. His residence in the United States had made him intensely British. He bitterly resented the Anglophobia of a

section of the United States press. Charles A. Dana of the New York
*Sun* was his pet hate. Dana one day wrote an editorial in which were
these words:

> England, the pigeon-livered, white-lipped coward among nations;
> the truculent bully and herself assassin of the feeble; the cringing
> bootlicking flunkey of the strong.

"J. P." replied, under the heading "Dana in a Snapshot," as
follows:

> Dana, the treacherous cut-throat of American journalism; the
> guttersnipe of the New York newspaper world; the backer of political
> thieves, harlots and murderers; the dirty slanderer of better men than
> he can ever hope to be; the marplot engaged in seducing foreigners
> from their allegiance to friendly governments; the irascible villifier
> of representative American statesmen; the rowdy critic and hoary-
> headed old sinner; the hell-begotten devil of the anti-British colony
> of the Republic.
>
> Dana, the reptile whose hiss is always heard at the heels of
> Morality and Decency. Dana, the smell issuing from the excrement
> of Yankee jingoism; Dana, the putrid mouthpiece of the rotten inner
> circles of crime-steeped Tammany.

Such editorializing was not uncommon at the turn of the century!

Of the three partners who owned the Galt *Reporter,* I liked Tom
Sears best. Tom was as kindly and soft spoken as Jaffray was brusque.
A fine gentleman, he seldom lost his temper, and was a wonder at
straightening out difficulties common to small town papers. His work
was primarily in the business office, selling advertising and job printing, and, most difficult of all, finding enough money to pay wages.

Sears stayed with the Galt *Reporter* until 1897, when he bought
the Welland *Telegraph.* Later he sold the Welland paper to his
son Frank and Louis Blake Duff. When he left journalism, Tom
joined the sales staff of the Toronto Type Foundry. Year after year
he made the round of Ontario newspapers and printing plants. A
genial fellow, he had bridge-playing friends in every town. His son,
William, later became president of Sears, Ltd., a Toronto printing
machinery firm.

The biggest scoop the Galt *Reporter* scored in my time, and
probably ever since, happened on March 17, 1897, the day of the fight
for the world's heavyweight title between American "Gentleman
Jim" Corbett, the champion, and Australian Bob Fitzsimmons, the
challenger.

Never in my memory has there been a fight which caused so much excitement. Corbett, fast afoot and an able jabber, had won his title by wearing out poor, tired, old John L. Sullivan. Fitzsimmons was a heavy middleweight and also fast. The fight had an international aspect—the British Empire against the United States. Many loyal Canadians were, however, backing Corbett.

The *Reporter* was a small town daily. It had just emerged from the weekly field, and had no business to try to handle such a big news story as that fight. Nor could it afford to. Galt would have to wait until the Toronto papers arrived the next day to learn who had won.

However, next door to the *Reporter* was the office of the Great Northwest Telegraph Company, in charge of Miss Nellie Kyle, a bespectacled and sometimes sharp-tongued operator. The partition between the two offices was wood, and quite thin. Ordinarily the ceaseless chatter of the Morse messages travelling over the leased wires was an unmitigated nuisance. The day of the big fight it was a gift from the gods.

Editor and ex-telegrapher Jaffray sat himself at a table close to the wall. As the story of the fight passed through on the wires from Carson City, Nevada, to Toronto and Montreal, he wrote it down round by round in longhand, and handed it to his partner Sears. Tom rushed it to the pullbox which carried copy to the composing room. There I was waiting to run it to the typesetting machine. The type was then hustled to the empty column in the page form on the Wharfedale press.

Little other work was done in the *Reporter* office that day. Sears and Knowles eagerly looked over Jaffray's shoulders as he transcribed the dots and dashes. Upstairs the whole composing room staff crowded around the typesetting machine to read what they could of the battle's progress.

At first it looked like a Corbett victory. An early knockout seemed near. But "Fitz" fought back desperately. After the tenth round Corbett began to tire.

Jaffray was a Corbett fan; Sears was for Fitzsimmons. I can still hear Tom Sears' shout of triumph up the composing room chute when the flash came that Fitzsimmons had delivered the famous solar plexus punch which ended the fight.

The partners came up the stairs on the run. One of the alternate headings I had set in advance was dropped in the form, the column was spaced out and the quoins tightened. A moment later the big press began to wheeze, groan, and bump, and the papers to come through.

Within five minutes of the word of Fitzsimmons' victory the *Reporter* sporting extra was on the street. We were the first paper in Canada to publish the news. None of the big city dailies was able to get to press as quickly since they had to stereotype their pages after making them up.

To his dying day "J. P." used to brag about that amazing feat in small town journalism. The ethics of it were never discussed. Later he may have paid a fee for the wire service he tapped, but not a big one. Small town newspapers were never big money makers in those days, and the Toronto dailies probably did not think it worth while to begin legal proceedings over the *Reporter*'s "steal." The goodwill of the Galt newspaper was worth keeping. Besides, no special harm had been done.

In a letter written many years afterwards, "J. P." claimed that it was Miss Kyle, the Great Northwest Telegraph operator, who, herself, had transcribed the fight story from the wires. If she did, then all I can say is that she was very clever at imitating Jaffray's handwriting.

# 4 «««

## *The Mighty Mite*

SOLE SURVIVOR of the newspapermen with whom I worked in Galt is Louis Blake Duff.

Duff is brief in stature but not in statement. His square cranium, with its typically Irish features, is unusual not only in appearance but content.

As a humourist Louis Blake Duff may not rank with Stephen Leacock, but as an after-dinner speaker he more than holds his own. Leacock chewed his words, was difficult to understand, and telegraphed his jokes through his twinkling eyes. Duff's wittiest quips come from a countenance as sober as an undertaker's. His are the histrionic gifts of a trained actor.

I first met him when he was gathering news for the Galt *Reporter* and on two occasions substituted for him while he was on holidays. My proof reading was never faultless and Duff tells of a typographical error for which I may or may not have been responsible.

For the personals column of the *Reporter* one day was written a simple item about the visit of a local resident to the nearby town of Dunnville. Somehow or other, however, it appeared this way in print:

Mrs. Henry Spencer Howell is spending a few days with her son Lawrie who is in the Bank of Commerce at *Dungville*.

Mr. Henry Spencer Howell, an incorrigible wag, bought up all the spare papers in town and mailed them to friends. His aged mother, however, was humiliated, and came in the next day to see Arthur Donaldson. No printed apology could be devised which would not make things worse. Arthur was, therefore, much relieved when the old lady finally told him that she, herself, did not mind so much, but "poor Henry" was grief-stricken over it.

Louis Blake Duff began his career as a schoolteacher but, after four years of verbally admonishing the young and a few months of research for a shorthand expert in the city of Toronto, he was invited by Blake Elliott of the Wingham *Times* to manage his weekly temporarily. Duff tells it this way:

I took the first train so as not to give him a chance to change his mind for I longed to get on a newspaper. I was in full charge from Easter to Labour Day when Blake returned. I wrote the news, the editorials, and most of the advertisements. I read proofs, edited the country correspondence, collected the bills, and even pulled the lever of the Washington hand press. By Labour Day I knew all about every phase of newspaper work—and more.

Then I went to the Stratford *Beacon,* owned in those days by W. M. O'Beirne. He was a short-sighted man who wore thick glasses and could not see what a jewel he had. I heard "J. P." Jaffray of the Galt *Reporter* calling, and moved to Galt the day of Queen Victoria's funeral, lightening the gloom of the town's official mourning. Four years of unalloyed happiness followed. I really learned something from Jaffray. I never knew anyone who ate, drank and slept his town like "J. P." Galt was the centre of his universe. He knew all the Galtonians who had gone to the four corners of the earth and were making names for themselves. Every step they made up the ladder was a joy to him.

But one day Tom Sears, who once owned a share in the Galt *Reporter,* came to town and suggested that I go to Welland and edit the *Telegraph* which his son Frank was running for him. Six months after I landed, on January 1, 1905, I went into partnership with Frank Sears. We bought the plant for $10,000, mostly on wind. Two years later Frank took ill, and I bought him out with more wind. The Lord tempered the two gales to the shorn lamb, and I survived.

That Welland *Telegraph* episode lasted for twenty-one years and was very happy and even successful in a way. But in October of 1926 a big car filled with lawyers arrived in town. They coveted my paper and, at three o'clock that afternoon, I was sitting out on the curb, unemployed for the first time in half a century.

But Duff was not idle long. He organized, successfully operated, and sold the Niagara Finance Company; assembled one of the finest libraries on this continent on the development of printing and the press; authored an unending succession of witty pamphlets; and, in *The County Kerchief,* published a full-length book on the history of hanging and other forms of capital punishment.

But pioneer Canadian editor and publisher Louis Blake Duff has lost none of his journalistic flair. When in October of 1952 the University of Western Ontario conferred on him, along with two others, the honorary degree Doctor of Laws, he solemnly suggested that universities should do more than merely hand to those so honoured a piece of parchment.

"Why not," he asked, "give each a button such as the Rotarians and the Elks wear? Something that will identify us wherever we go? The public will look at the buttons and ask about them. Then we can pleasantly explain. The Republican party has spent five million dollars in the United States for 'I like Ike' buttons. All I am asking the board of regents to do is to provide three buttons at a cost of 75 cents. Surely scholars are more worthy than politicians. A scholar meets every problem with an open mind, a politician with an open mouth."

Canadian journalism found one of its brightest ornaments in this mite of a man whose wit filled a whole countryside.

# 5 «‹‹

## *"Whiskers" and "Whiskey Geordie"*

GALT IN MY TIME had its quota of unconscious as well as conscious humourists.

"Whiskers" Knight, one of the best self-advertisers I ever knew, frequently furnished paragraphs for the paper and laughs for its readers. His real name was "Joe" and he and his negro rival, Jim Moore, were competitors for the town's backhouse cleaning business.

Unlike Jim, who sometimes got drunk and landed in police court, "Whiskers'" sole trouble was his temper. When the boys snowballed him, or stoned and upset the barrels on his wagon, he administered his own justice. He was fleet of foot and few were the miscreants who escaped without a sore bottom or red ears.

"Whiskers" was so called because of his flaming red brush goatee, and his hair was of the same brilliant hue. Six days of the week it was tousled, but on Sundays and on other special occasions, it was carefully oiled, combed, and rigidly plastered down.

Sunday was the big day for "Whiskers." He drove with his family to Knox Church, the most fashionable kirk in the town. The weather-beaten bony nag that pulled his sewage cart during the week on Sundays drew an ancient leather-upholstered Victoria. And "Whiskers" was scrubbed so clean, he literally shone. On his head sat an old Christie. A Prince Albert coat reached almost to his knees. Surmounting a white shirt was a high, white, saw-edged collar which rubbed his ears. The goatee emerged where the collar tabs turned down, almost hiding a scarlet tie. His trousers were creased down the sides; his boots highly polished. So attired, he led his family in a grand parade each Sunday morning to the Knight pew, right down front.

16

But it was at funerals that "Whiskers" really sparkled. He did business with the town's best families and he never forgot to honour his customers. He and his wife were always there in their Sunday best, edging their dilapidated Victoria into the heart of the procession.

"Whiskers" lived in the days before there was much talk about "inferiority complexes." We used to think him bumptious. But now I am certain he had an urge to rise to better things. His daily work, though honest and necessary, gave him a sense of inferiority, and when he put on his best clothes and drove in a funeral procession to the cemetery, who was to say he was not as good as the best among us. Indeed one of his sons proved that to be so. He became the manager of one of New York's larger department stores.

Another one of our town characters was "Whiskey Geordie." Geordie Waddie was a confirmed alcoholic, but his wife, Jean, was ever loyal to him.

One night Geordie appeared at the family domicile not only inebriated but accompanied.

"Mercy me, Geordie," remonstrated Jean. "What's that ye've got wi' ye?"

"I hae got a horse, Jean. Ye ken I aye wanted a horse."

"But Geordie," remonstrated his spouse, "where on airth are ye going to keep it?"

"I'm going to keep it in the kitchen, Jean."

"But, Geordie, there's nae room in the kitchen for a horse."

"It's a cool nicht, Jean, and the puir beast must hae shelter somewhere."

They eased the horse into the wee kitchen and it ended up against the stove.

"Ye see for yersel, Geordie," said Jean. "It'll never dae in here."

Geordie was forced to admit it. He tried to get the horse out, but could not turn it round. There was not room.

"We could see naething tae it but to tak' doon the wall," said Jean to her neighbours the next day. "But I told Geordie to go and get that man Turnbull who was awfu' guid wi' horses. So Geordie went for that man Turnbull, and, dae ye ken, he got it oot in five meenits. Wad ye ken how he got it oot? I never would hae thocht o' it. *He backed it oot.* Oh, a clever man wi' a horse."

Another time Geordie fell on his back and was not able to regain his feet. His bosom pal, also the worse for liquor, attempted to help him up, but failed. Then said he, "Geordie, ah canna get ye up, so I'll jist lie down beside ye."

Rev. R. E. Knowles of Galt put one of the Geordie stories into his novel *St. Cuthbert's*. Mr. Knowles, himself, was the minister in the tale.

Geordie's wife sent the minister to the tavern in search of the prodigal. When the two were out on the street, Geordie paused and said under his breath: "It's a sair shock and it'll kill the wife."

"Your wife will forgive you, Geordie," began the minister, "and if this will only teach . . ."

Geordie's face showed that he had been sorely misunderstood.

"Forgie me! Forgie me! It's no me that she'll hae to forgie. Are ye no the meenister o' St. Cuthbert's? Ye canna deny that! I ken that fine. I kent ye as sune as ye came slippin' ben the tavern. I'm no what I micht be masel, but I dinna mak no profession; but to think that I'd catch my ain meenister hanging roon' a tavern at this time o' nicht. It'll kill the wife. She thocht the warld o' ye. Yere a wolf in sheep's clothes, and I'm sore at hairt the nicht. It maun hae a fearful hold on ye when ye come oot at sic an oor."

As they neared Geordie's home the drunken man turned to his minister.

"I want ye to promise me ane thing afore we part," he said. "It's for your ain guid I'm asking it."

"What is it?" asked the cleric.

"Ah want ye to sign the pledge," said Geordie.

And as they parted, Geordie offered the parson a sweetie, a peppermint lozenge, and as a final word this advice:

"Lie wi' yir back to the wife—and sip the sweetie—and breathe in to yersel'."

# 6 ⧏⧏

## *Pioneering the Talking Machine*

I HAD BEEN working on the Galt *Reporter* for a little over a year when I began to feel my oats. Three dollars a week, even in those days, didn't seem proper compensation for an "experienced" journalist. So I asked "J. P." Jaffray for a raise.

He refused. Two months later I resigned and went to Galt Business College for a course in shorthand and typewriting.

From my fifteen months at the *Reporter* and my stay at business college some legacies have remained through the years. My knowledge of "the case" has never wholly left me; I can still, theoretically, feed a Gordon press; and I have always used shorthand and still do. Transcribing notes may have slowed me up, but it has permitted much more accurate reporting than if I had relied, as do so many modern journalists, on memory and longhand.

To earn my way through business college, I capitalized on the latest wonder of the age—the talking machine. Father had purchased in 1897 one of the first gramophones to come into our part of Ontario. At the initial demonstration concert in Fraser's Hall, Galt, some sixty skeptical people gathered.

Father made an explanatory speech and left me the task of preparing for its audition the curious contraption with the huge, bell-mouthed horn. A steel spring had to be wound up carefully but fully by hand before each record was inserted. If the record was long, the spring lost its tension and distorted the sound.

The first number went off splendidly, and was greeted with loud and sustained applause. I began to wind for number two. I wound and wound. Suddenly "B-A-N-G!" The spring snapped. The concert was over and father gave the people their money back.

19

A new spring was secured after some days. Though I did not again appear in town, each week during the fall, winter and spring I gave concerts in country schoolhouses to earn money for my college fees. Two trips with a hired horse and buggy were required per concert. On the first, I got permission from school trustees and put up advertising bills. On the second, I gave the programme. Farmers and their families came from miles around and paid ten cents for adults and five cents for children to hear the talking wonder. My biggest net profit for one night was $8.50 and the lowest $2.75.

The long drive home through the lonely darkness often chilled the enthusiasm of a seventeen-year-old. But the gramophone and my business course had to be paid for.

# 7 ⋘

## Pattullo: "Colossus of Roads"

FEW SMALL TOWN newspapers in Canada ever boasted a more remarkable staff of editors and reporters than did the *Sentinel-Review* of Woodstock when I joined it on October 30, 1898.

Publisher, and member of the Provincial Legislature, Andrew Pattullo had a fight on his hands. The exclusive hold which his Liberal *Sentinel-Review* once had on the town and countryside had been challenged by a new daily, the *Express,* launched by D. W. Karn, a Woodstock organ manufacturer, and some of his Conservative friends. John Markey, editor of the *Sentinel-Review* and reporter Charles Hamlin had forsaken Pattullo and gone over to the new Tory enemy.

The Woodstock *Weekly Times* had also decided to throw its hat into the daily ring. Its publisher, Vaughan Francis, and its editor and reporter George W. Hunt, were experienced newspapermen.

Determined to drive out his competitors at any cost, Pattullo hired a super staff of writers—a group of men who in subsequent years attained top rank in the press and political life of Canada.

Pattullo reserved for himself the editorial page and also took an active part in the editorial and business management. As his city editor he chose a nephew, A. Balmer Watt, who, prior to his retirement in 1947, was for some forty years editor of the Edmonton *Journal.* One of his reporters was James Hunter who, after a term as private secretary to the Hon. James Sutherland, was later for three decades Deputy Minister of Public Works at Ottawa. Another reporter was Jack O'Higgins, destined to head his own advertising agency in Toronto.

From the Toronto *World,* to liven up local news stories, came Alf

Rubbra. Subsequently he became city editor of the Toronto *News* and, later still, a senior deskman on the Toronto *Star*. George R. Pattullo Jr., another nephew of the publisher and later a well known contributor to the *Saturday Evening Post,* was a fourth reporter. Directing the business end was Charles A. Abraham, a future advertising manager of the Toronto *Star,* who was, himself, succeeded at Woodstock by J. F. Mackay, years afterward the business manager of the Toronto *Globe.*

When these journalistic lights were turned on, Woodstock sat up and rubbed its eyes. Rubbra dug up long hidden scandals and wrote them in the racy style of the old Toronto *World.* Hunter, Pattullo, O'Higgins each produced his share of good copy. I put together daily two or three columns of sport.

Advertising revenues were threatened for a time but circulation mounted steadily. Before a year had passed the *Sentinel-Review* was in a stronger position than when it was first challenged. The *Times* fell by the wayside. Though still alive, the *Express* had shot its bolt. So expenses were cut and the *Sentinel-Review's* all-star staff reduced to normal size.

Pattullo, with his massive square head, high forehead, and penetrating eyes, was one of the finest newspapermen I ever knew. He had a brilliant mind, a terse and vigorous pen. Three years before I joined the *Sentinel-Review,* however, he had lost his wife, Isabel Balmer, a blow from which he never recovered. Almost wholly lacking in humour, he became highly nervous and subject to fits of depression.

Born in Caledon, Ontario, Andrew Pattullo grew up near Drumbo in Oxford County. He had an outstanding scholastic record. After attending grammar schools at Dundas and St. Catharines, he won a scholarship entitling him to three years at the University of London, England. After only one year abroad, however, ill health forced him to return to Canada where he joined the staff of the weekly Woodstock *Sentinel,* then owned by his brother George. Five years later, in 1880, Andrew Pattullo bought the paper and amalgamated it with the weekly Woodstock *Review.* The combined *Sentinel-Review* emerged as a daily in 1886 and soon attained a national reputation. Pattullo was for three successive years elected to the presidency of the Canadian Press Association but spurned numerous offers of metropolitan editorial chairs for the quieter life of his country town.

Yet his pen played a powerful part in shaping Ontario's political life. From the editorial page to the party arena was for him a short jump and an easy one. His ability as a campaign orator brought him invitations from all over Ontario and when, in 1896, Sir Oliver Mowat retired as the Provincial Liberal leader, Pattullo succeeded him as the member for North Oxford.

Andrew Pattullo was the father of the good roads movement in Ontario, and almost entirely responsible for the appointment of A. W. Campbell as the Province's first highways commissioner. Widely known as the "Colossus of Roads," his enthusiasm for improved traffic arteries, and his ability to present his arguments, made him a familiar figure on public platforms in many parts of North America.

He was also an authority on agricultural matters. For two terms he served as president of the Western Ontario Dairymen's Association, an unusual honour for a newspaper publisher.

For three successive terms Pattullo was elected to the Ontario legislature by the people of North Oxford and seemed surely to be headed for the cabinet. But on December 29, 1903, while I was a student at McMaster University, came the shocking news that Pattullo had killed himself in London, England. The *Sentinel-Review* had by then been sold to W. J. Taylor, and Pattullo had gone to England to take part in the Hon. Joseph Chamberlain's campaign for Imperial Preference. There he addressed a number of meetings but, exceedingly sensitive to newspaper criticism, in bad health, and his nerves near collapse, he could take it no longer.

The Pattullo suicide was a calamity in Woodstock and a national sensation. His was the third suicide among eminent Canadian journalists within a short period, following that of Nicholas Flood Davin of Winnipeg and Alexander Pirie of Dundas.

# 8 «««

## *I Walked in Free*

As A BOY the only way I could get into the Galt ball park was over or under the fence when the cops weren't looking. And father proved conclusively in our woodshed that such crimes do not pay!

But as the eighteen-year-old sports editor of the Woodstock *Sentinel-Review*, I was in clover. Not only could I walk in free but I could associate as an equal with the sports heroes of the day.

One I remember was Noah Brusso, a native of Brussels, Ontario, and one of the roughest, toughest, fightingest lacrosse players I have ever seen. I had a hand in bringing him from Galt to Woodstock as goalie and coach. Brusso never used his stick, but he was free with his fists on opponent and referee alike. Possibly I should not have been surprised to read a few years later that Noah, under his ring name of Tommy Burns, had defeated the giant negro Jack Johnston to become the heavyweight boxing champion of the world.

Another battler I remember, for more personal reasons, was Frank Norcrum, a Texas Indian, who pitched for the Woodstock club in the Canadian League. Norcrum taught me one of the basic lessons of journalism—it is much safer to call an athlete "yellow" from the shelter of a grandstand than it is to put the same charge into print in your own column.

Norcrum disliked hard work and lacked a fighting heart and, following a game in which he apparently quit deliberately when things went against him, I told the readers of the *Sentinel-Review* that the big Texan was "yellow." But that was my colour, not his, for the next two weeks. He boasted publicly that he would "cut my heart out," and I spent nearly as much time dodging as I did reporting. Finally the local police warned him to "lay off or leave town." Shortly afterward he was given his release by the local club, and I breathed a lot easier.

My education in objective reporting continued with my appointment as official scorer for the Canadian Baseball League. It was a short-lived job, ending with the collapse of the league two months after it began, but I discovered that most ball players have their own ideas how their plays should be scored.

It was one night in Brantford, however, that I received my most memorable lesson on the desirability of maintaining, as a reporter, a strictly neutral position. Rivalry between the Woodstock and Brantford hockey teams was intense. Fist fights between fans as well as players featured every game. And those were the days when there were no nets between the goal posts and the goal umpire was the sole judge of whether or not a team had scored. On this particular evening, shot after shot went through the Brantford posts but the home town umpires allowed not a goal. Umpires were changed several times at Woodstock's demand but still no tallies were recorded.

I was standing right behind the Brantford goal late in the game when the puck passed cleanly through the posts. I turned, expecting to see the umpire's hand go up. He merely shouted "no goal." I was mad and did not hesitate to call him the fanciest names in my vocabulary. If his friends had not held him back, and urged him to "leave the kid alone," I would have been pulverized. The goal umpire for Brantford that night was "Gander" Sherritt, amateur heavyweight boxing champion of Canada who was later killed while serving with the Dominion's forces in the Boer War.

The final score was 7-4 for Brantford but Woodstock had its revenge on home ice the following week with a 16-1 count. Just at that time William Jennings Bryan, the Great Commoner and perennial Democratic candidate, was running for the presidency of the United States on a platform of "sixteen to one." He was advocating that silver be freely coined in that ratio—sixteen silver dollars to one of gold. I wrote Mr. Bryan telling him of Woodstock's 16-1 victory and expressing the hope that it was a good omen for him. Within a few days from Lincoln, Nebraska, came the following reply:

March 4, 1899

My Dear Sir:

Your favour to hand with paper. Thanks for your kindness. As you are doubtless a young man I shall use this incident to enforce what I regard as an important thing for young men to learn, namely:

that success comes from attaching yourself to an idea. You know my name not because of any extraordinary ability on my part, but because of my advocacy of the restoration of bi-metallism in the United States at the ratio of 16 to 1 without waiting for the aid or consent of any other nation. While I am opposed to increasing the ratio between gold and silver, I will not complain if your club defeats its opponent next time by a score of 32 to 1.

Very truly yours,

W. J. Bryan

But my first year as a cub reporter at Woodstock was not confined solely to sports. The one incident which today remains most clearly etched on my memory relates not to mayhem in the sports arena but to what may well have been a case of murder on the gallows.

In the autumn of 1898 I was sent to the London, Ontario, jail with another Woodstock reporter to cover the hanging of "Peg-leg" Brown. Police Constable Toohey of the London force had been shot to death at midnight in the Grand Trunk Railway freight yards in an attempt to arrest a man suspected of having made an attack on a little girl. The killer was a "peg-leg." All over Ontario suspected cripples were rounded up, among them Brown, who best fitted the description given by Toohey before he died.

Though Brown maintained to the end that he was 200 miles away at the time of the murder, he was tried, convicted, and sentenced to death. He was a Negro, a wanderer, without friends or relatives.

As we went to the jail to get permits to witness the execution, from "Peg-leg's" cell came the music of a gospel hymn. The condemned Negro's powerful baritone rang high above the voices of Evangelist Griggs and the Salvation Army lasses who were with him through the night, alternately praying and singing. Again and again Brown sang "Hide me, O my Saviour hide," "This is my story, this is my song," and "O touch the hem of His garment."

I too was restless that night. Up at 5.30 a.m. for a hasty breakfast, we arrived at the jail an hour later. Hymns and prayers still came from Brown's cell.

At seven o'clock, the Rev. Dr. Robert Johnston, a tall, black-bearded Presbyterian minister, a giant mentally as well as physically, appeared. His mission to Ottawa seeking a reprieve and a new trial had failed.

To us reporters he delivered a passionate protest against the impending hanging. I took it in shorthand and I still have my notes.

I want to say a word of protest against this overstraining of justice in the case of a man against whom the crime of murder as described by no statute in the British law has been proved. I believe him innocent of wrong doing, yet justice will require his life at the hands of those who take it. God forgive them.

At 7.35 there arrived at the jail a man of middle age, medium stout, with an expressionless face. It was Radcliffe, the hangman for most executions of that period, carrying a parcel under his arm which I sensed to be the rope.

Under a dark and sodden sky we stood in the courtyard and waited. The singing and the prayers in the death cell alone broke the silence. Suddenly they stopped. Then through the dimly lit corridors of the jail came the sound of moving feet and the sharp clack-clack of a peg-leg on the stone floor.

An iron door opened. Out came Sheriff Cameron, then Rev. Dr. Johnston, his head bent low. Next the "peg-leg." He walked firmly. He looked us over unconcernedly. His eyes swept the yard. He saw the scaffold, braced himself, and turned toward it. His arms were strapped to his sides. Two turnkeys steadied him as he climbed the stairs and disappeared from sight behind the board wall at one side of the scaffold.

At 8 a.m. Rev. Dr. Johnston began in a broken voice to recite the Lord's Prayer. As he came to "For Thine is the Kingdom," Radcliffe pulled the trap and the Negro fell to his death. We heard but could not see. Simultaneously there was a flash of lightning and a loud clap of thunder.

Tears streaming down his face, Dr. Johnston concluded his prayer. Then stepping forward, his face uplifted and his long arms stretched toward Heaven, he cried: "God forgive us and forgive this country!"

"Peg-leg's" last words on the scaffold were, "If it be pleasing to Thee, O Lord, have mercy on my soul."

I wrote that story only once on paper, but I have re-written it time and time again in my heart. Reporting, even for an eighteen-year-old, is not all fun.

# 9 ⋘

## Back to School

ALTHOUGH I had little occasion for personal contact with *Sentinel-Review* editor and publisher Andrew Pattullo, he showed a kindly interest in his young sports editor and much of what I learned about journalism stems from his sage counsel. Noted for his complete mastery of any subject on which he chose to write or speak, he made it a rule that his reporters should never put pencil to paper until they were absolutely certain of all the facts.

When I started with Mr. Pattullo I was paid five dollars a week. Allowing for room and board, that left two dollars for clothing, laundry, amusements, and treating my girl.

Six months later, I was given an additional dollar a week along with some excellent advice from the boss—"be thrifty."

In mid-September, after I had put in nearly a year on the *Sentinel-Review*, I received a letter from J. P. Jaffray suggesting I return to Galt as a reporter at six dollars weekly. My attempt to use this as a lever to get a raise to eight dollars at Woodstock was ill-timed. Pattullo, quite rightly, did not consider me indispensable and suggested I accept the offer of a job on the Galt *Reporter*.

But I didn't want to go home. So I swallowed my pride and asked to be kept on for a while at six dollars a week until I could find work elsewhere. Visions of Winnipeg and Chicago swam in my nineteen-year-old head. But my parents had other ideas. They suggested that, if I would return to high school and later go on to university, they would help as they could.

So, in October, 1899, with board and tuition at four dollars a week, I became a student at Woodstock College, a Baptist secondary school for boys.

For years there had been ill feeling in Woodstock between town and college boys. The college lads, being outsiders, had more glamour and were more successful in dating the town girls. This bad blood led to the most memorable event of my two years at the school.

The collegians customarily held a Hallowe'en parade. That year, 1899, the town boys planned to break it up. They laid in stocks of rotten apples and tomatoes. However, we were tipped off that they were going to treat us roughly and prepared to meet them, arming ourselves with pieces of rubber hose and lengths of broomstick. Protected by senior students on horseback, and with strong-armed huskies front and rear, we set out. Less than half a mile from the college we ran into a tomato barrage, and before we reached down town other skirmishes had taken place.

At the town square, where we were surrounded by a great mob, an overripe pumpkin bounced off the head of a collegian. One of our chaps swung his rubber hose on an innocent spectator, splitting his ear. This enraged the town boys and we decided to make a tactical retreat. After we crossed the bridge over the railway on our way back to the campus, we were showered with jagged coal cinders and suffered a number of minor casualties. One policeman pulled out a gun but it was snatched from his hands by a college student. It was a merry evening!

First thing the next morning, to make sure that the College got a fair break, I was down at the *Sentinel-Review* office to write the story of what proved to be our last Hallowe'en parade, for twelve collegians and one townsman had required medical treatment.

My first dip into college journalism was at Woodstock. In my final year I was appointed joint editor of the *Oracle*, published once a month by the Senior Literary Society by being read aloud. I also kept my fingers in printer's ink by writing a weekly column of College News for the *Sentinel-Review* for which I was paid fifty cents an issue. With the addition of a serialized history of the College in the second year the ante was raised to seventy-five cents. That money was mighty welcome for my father was even then well acquainted with the dollar shortage.

Principal of the College at that time was Abraham Lincoln McCrimmon. His parents made no mistake in naming him after the great American president. There was much of Lincoln in him.

Big in every way, his vigorous six-foot frame was topped by square shoulders and a strong head and face. At Toronto University he had been an all round athlete, and at Woodstock he encouraged the students to play games by joining in them himself. Not only was he a first class rugby football half back, but he played a good game of cricket, and was quick with hands and feet on the tennis court.

The first time I played rugby against him, I thought it wise, since he was the principal, not to tackle him too heavily. He had no like scruples. When I picked up a loose ball and started to run with it he bowled me over with the savage gentleness of a locomotive.

Later I had my revenge in a cricket game between town and College. I was not good enough for the College eleven, but when the town team arrived one man short I was asked to play for them. McCrimmon nearly always scored fifty or more runs and when College came to bat, he was one of the first pair in. I was playing in deep field where it was thought I could do little damage. The principal hit one of the first balls bowled a mighty blow. It came straight for me so fast I could not get out of the way. The ball crashed through my hands into my stomach. I grabbed and held on. McCrimmon was out for a duck's egg on my first and only cricket catch.

But A. L. McCrimmon was much more than a sportsman. He was a stern disciplinarian. Not even the boldest boy enjoyed facing those beetling eyebrows when summoned to the principal's office. Seldom did he use the strap. With a few words he could dissolve braggadocio into tears. Those who did not admire him, feared him. He was an ideal headmaster.

McCrimmon's standards were high and he made us acquainted with them in chapel or private talks. No sturdier Baptist lived in all Canada. As principal of Woodstock College he was expected to visit the churches and plead the cause of Christian education. An eloquent preacher, his vocabulary was large and multi-syllabled, and words poured from his lips like a mountain torrent.

His classroom subjects were classics and history. Believing in old-fashioned methods, he taught us a multitude of trick memory aids which later helped in the field of journalism.

Four other Woodstock teachers stand out in my memory: Neil S. McKechnie, vice-principal, and teacher of English, a gracious but firm Christian gentleman; Arthur M. Overholt, brilliant teacher of mathematics, who gave as much care to developing slow minds as to the quick, and afterwards became the beloved principal of Brantford Collegiate; J. W. Russell, science master, known to us as "Scrape" because of a mannerism of rubbing his hand on his chin as he talked, who, after not too successfully prospecting and developing a silver mine near Cobalt, became the popular and practical professor of mineralogy at the University of Western Ontario; and D. K. Clark, who organized and conducted Ontario's first manual training department, and incidentally taught modern languages.

Out of school for three years, I was considerably behind my classmates of the Junior year but I was also three years older than most of them, and therefore had a better idea of why I was there. Because of my age and the fact that I had so much to catch up, I was allowed to stay up an hour or more after the other chaps had gone to bed. With this advantage of longer study hours, I was awarded, on graduation, the Governor-General's medal. I tell this only because it brought me to the attention of Chancellor Wallace of McMaster University, and led to my taking an arts course there before turning once again to full-time journalism.

# 10 ⋘

## The Last Post

MY TWO YEARS at Woodstock College paid off. Following graduation
in the summer of 1901 I got a reportorial job on the Hamilton
*Morning Post,* and the salary was nine dollars a week—when there
was money enough.

The *Post* had been launched only that spring. Hamilton at that
time had two other newspapers, the Conservative *Spectator* and the
Liberal *Times,* both evening dailies. Hamiltonians were, however,
dependent for their morning news on the Toronto press—the *Globe,*
the *Mail and Empire,* and the *World.*

Even then called "The Ambitious City," Hamilton had among
its citizenry men who felt it a disgrace that the budding metropolis
on the west end of Lake Ontario had no morning paper of its own.
Prominent among them was a Conservative lawyer named Scott who
organized the Morning Post Publishing Company and became its first
and only president.

Business manager of the new paper was Jim Livingstone, publisher of the lively neighbouring weekly, the Grimsby *Independent.*
Livingstone belonged to the old school of journalism. He was a
keen sportsman and an assiduous follower of the ponies. He worked
when it was absolutely necessary, but he felt that the best way to run
a newspaper was to hire some good men and let them do it while
he scurried around to collect enough money for their wages.

Editor-in-chief of the *Morning Post* was B. K. Sandwell, many
years after the presiding genius of Toronto's *Saturday Night.* "B. K."
was young and keen, and had abundant energy, a scholar's brain, a
brilliant wit, a fine mastery of English and a nose for news.

If its business management had been as efficient as its editorial direction, the *Post* would have lived longer. But the advertising competition of evening dailies, then as now, was virtually prohibitive.

Two stories stay with me from that summer in Hamilton, and each played a part in my decision never to become a police reporter. My daily routine included a call to police headquarters just before midnight. One evening a woman, her throat badly cut, was received at city hospital. The police had, at that time, no lead on the cause.

I started for the slum area near the Bay to investigate. As I climbed the steps of the house where the slashing had allegedly occurred, a second storey window was opened and a gruff voiced, drunken man called out: "What the hell!" Without identifying myself, and in a tone which must have sounded much firmer to him than it did to me, I demanded to know what had happened. Apparently believing he was talking to a representative of the police, the inebriated man blurted out the story. I ran back to the *Post* with a first-rate scoop. The next morning, however, a *Spectator* reporter called at the same house for more details. This time the man, still intoxicated, chased the reporter a full block wielding a big butcher knife.

Violence also figured in the second incident. Editor Sandwell had asked me to follow up a paragraph in the rival *Spectator* about the coming police court appearance of a well known, but unidentified, clergyman who had been making a nuisance of himself in city parks. To my consternation I found that the man charged was the occupant of the next room in my boarding house and the landlady's brother-in-law.

At first I declined the assignment. But, believing that my friend and neighbour must have suddenly become mentally unbalanced, I later wrote a sympathetic background story. Shortly after its publication, I was assisting the police in their search for an attempted suicide. We came across a man, lying apparently dead, in the city's east-end park. Clutched in his hand was the newspaper story I had written. It was my friend from the boarding house. Overwhelmed by the disgrace which he had brought to his family, he had tried to take his own life. I felt like a murderer. Fortunately, however, he was still alive and, after a brief stay in hospital, recovered and was committed for some months to a mental institution.

But even more exciting than anything that happened to me on the police beat that summer was Friday night in the *Morning Post* office on James Street across from the City Hall. Would we or would we not get paid this week? The longer the paper lived, the tougher it was to get money. After the first few weeks, the *Post* had no bank credit. Business manager Jim Livingstone really worked Thursdays and Fridays. He collected accounts, sold advance advertising at a discount for cash, and often borrowed from friends. More than once the presses were plated and ready but not a wheel turned until "the ghost walked." Sometimes there was a delay of an hour or more until Jim came in with the money with which to pay the mechanical staff.

The men in the plant always got their envelopes first. They had a union. If there wasn't enough cash to go around, the editorial, business, and circulation staffs were asked to wait till next morning, next Monday, or sometime next week. These deferred payments became a standing Hamilton joke and the directors ordered Livingstone to get his finances in better shape. He quit. A search for a successor proved fruitless. So president Scott tried to carry on by himself. The first week he managed to find enough money but on the following Friday there were no pay envelopes. The mechanics went on strike. He pleaded with them to accept next day his personal cheque to which they finally agreed.

I left the *Post's* employ September 25 with the sum of $31.50, more than three weeks' salary, still owing. The cashier finally scraped together $18 in cash and promised to send the balance by mail. It never came, and since I was hoping to put myself through college that fall, it did not enhance my opinion of morning newspapers.

Mr. Scott's enterprise did not long survive my departure. On October 5, 1901, after six struggling months, its creditors sounded the last post.

# 11 ⋘

## *Four Years on Forty-five Dollars*

ANDREW PATTULLO's injunction "be thrifty," delivered with my $6 weekly pay envelope from the Woodstock *Sentinel-Review,* and the financial vagaries of my summer on the *Morning Post* were good training for the next four years.

In my last term at Woodstock College, Dr. O. C. S. Wallace, the Chancellor of McMaster University in Toronto, had urged me to continue my education in an arts course. "Save all you can and I shall keep in touch with you," he said.

As my stay with the *Post* neared its end, however, I had written Chancellor Wallace pointing out that my accumulated savings of a mere $45 made it quite impossible to think of university. He replied at once, brief and to the point: "Bring your $45 and we will see you through!"

That promise was kept. A new post of assistant librarian and university postman was created. I was its first occupant at $50 per year. Dr. Wallace paid me at time rates for a host of other small jobs, such as folding and mailing circulars. Several scholarships came along and, at the end of the first year, there was actually a small balance in the bank. A Woodstock lawyer friend, S. G. MacKay and my uncle, James Ryrie, made me interest-free loans. On graduation, I owed only $400—a sum I was able to repay within a year.

During my first summer at university, I worked as a commercial traveller for my father. Believing it would benefit my health, I decided, the second summer, to try a farm job instead. One day was enough. My farmer-employer waked me while it was yet dark and asked me to pitch a load of hay out of the mow before breakfast. When, at the end of that day, he suggested it would be wise if I tried some other way of making a living, I was too exhausted to argue the point. I went back to travelling for Dad till college re-opened.

Most interesting and profitable for me, journalistically, was the work I was able to do on the *McMaster University Monthly*. For the first three of my four years I was class reporter and, in the final year, editor of "Around the Hall," a department which covered the major happenings, except sports, of the whole university. I also contributed occasional articles to the literary section. After graduation, I edited for some years the "Our Graduates" column, and for two decades represented arts graduates on the university senate.

While our class of 1905 was small, among its thirty-three members —thirty men and three women—were many destined to reach top rungs in national and international life. Among them were W. G. Carpenter, D. L. McLaurin, and George W. Gorman, educational leaders of western Canada; Rev. Dr. J. B. McLaurin, head for years of the Canadian Baptist missionary work in India and later Foreign Mission Secretary for his Church; Rev. Dr. D. A. McGregor, head of the religious education department of the Protestant Episcopal Church of the United States; Ephraim Viens, director of the testing laboratories of Canada's federal Department of Public Works; and Cyrus S. Eaton of Cleveland, multi-millionaire investment banker and industrial promoter. We argued and lived together in an atmosphere which did much to mould my future thinking. And there too I met, as a member of the arts class of 1907, Eva Wilkins, the daughter of a Toronto wholesale merchant, who, in September of 1908, became my wife and later the mother of our two boys, Bill and Tom.

We had an inspiring faculty.

Dr. Wallace, Nova Scotian by birth, tall, athletic, his handsome face surmounted by white and tight curly hair, as Chancellor of McMaster from 1896 to 1905 laid well the foundations on which the university grew to Canada-wide recognition. His students were his children and he gave them his heart.

Dr. Alexander C. MacKay, first Registrar and later Chancellor, was our professor of mathematics. An extraordinary teacher, he was persuaded following retirement to plan the buildings and curriculum of Toronto's first technical school. Dean of Arts, professor of English and apostle of Browning, Walter S. W. McLay; Dr. George Cross, whose inspiring history lectures were far from book-bound; Dean of Theology, Dr. Jones Hughes Farmer, a man whose spirit was as large as his body was small; each lives with me still.

The year I graduated, Chancellor Wallace accepted a call to the pastorate of Westmount Baptist Church in Montreal. His declining years were spent as minister of the Eutaw Place Baptist Church in Baltimore. Before he died, he became totally blind but such was his spirit and energy that he taught himself to use the typewriter and regularly contributed articles to both the religious and secular press. I visited him several times in his Baltimore home and it was there he spoke a word I shall always treasure. "I have helped many young men," said the Chancellor of my university, "but you are one of the very few who have remembered."

"Bring your $45 and we will see you through!" It would have been a very poor reporter who would forget the author of a statement like that.

# 12 ⋘

## *John Barleycorn Again*

IT WAS A LETTER to Sir Wilfrid Laurier about the evils of whiskey
which started me on the road to journalism, and it was John Barleycorn
who introduced me to the Toronto *Star,* my newspaper home for
twenty-nine years.

Early in my course at McMaster University I had gone to see
J. E. Atkinson, publisher of Toronto's youngest evening daily. My
diary tells me that "he as good as promised me a job" when I
graduated, and "is a very fine fellow."

But in the meantime the continuance of my college education
depended on summer earnings. At the end of my third year, despite
a deep-seated antipathy toward selling anything, I signed up with the
publishing house of King Richardson to peddle, door to door, through
Alberta a book entitled *Prophets, Priests and Kings.*

Only ten days later, however, I was able, with considerable relief,
to call off the contract. A message came that the *Star's* city editor,
Colin C. Campbell, wished to see me. One of the *Star's* more brilliant
staff writers, a man with a big following because of his ability to
write sob sister verse on human interest topics, went on a prolonged
spree. He had been fired several times before, but this time it was to
be for keeps. Of course, it wasn't, but in the interval another reporter
was needed. So, when exams were over a few days later, I was to start
at $12 per week, hours 7.30 a.m. to 4.30 p.m. if lucky, and Saturday
afternoons off.

The *Star* was then a struggling upstart in the crowded Toronto
newspaper field. Regarded with editorial contempt by its rivals, it
had, nonetheless, begun to gain both readership and advertising
under the shrewd management of J. E. Atkinson. In the five years
since he had been persuaded to leave the Montreal *Herald* to assume

the post of publisher, the *Star's* circulation had climbed from a meagre 7,000 to nearly 31,000.

It was then being published in the old *Saturday Night* building on Adelaide Street, with pressroom in the basement, five or six editorial offices on the second floor, and private quarters for Atkinson and his secretary, Charles E. Fortier, later to become advertising director of the Bell Telephone Company. Business offices were located in a building on the southeast corner of Yonge and Adelaide Streets. W. C. R. Harris, Charles Abraham and W. L. Argue were respectively business, advertising and circulation managers.

Atkinson had gathered about him a notable staff of editors and writers, some of whom became nationally known in after years. Editor-in-chief was Joseph T. Clark; city editor, Colin C. Campbell; sports editor, W. A. Hewitt; assistant sports editor, Lou E. Marsh; financial editor and occasional poet, H. D. Carman. Special features from Ottawa were contributed by the brilliant writer, Harry Franklin Gadsby. John R. Bone was senior reporter; W. E. Plewman, municipal reporter; and the reportorial staff included Jimmy Simpson, afterwards mayor of Toronto; Arthur Roebuck, later attorney general of Ontario, member of parliament, and now senator; Robert K. Mearns, Charlie Raymond, Harold Adamson, William Clark and William Wiggins (still with the *Star* after half a century). Staff artist was Charles W. Jefferys, who was to attain distinction for his brilliant work in visualizing Canada's past with pen and brush. Thomas McGillicuddy did special writing.

It was a good staff and I was proud to belong to it although much of my first summer's work as a cub reporter was confined to the novice's job of covering the churches. Progressively, however, I developed a Saturday religious column.

Two incidents and only two remain in my memory from those months. The first relates to the Archbishop of Canterbury whom I interviewed when he arrived in Toronto one day in 1904 with the late J. Pierpont Morgan, international banker. I was much more impressed by the enormous size and purple colour of Mr. Morgan's bulbous nose than I was by any of the attributes of the church dignitary. "He deserves to have money to make up for it" was my diary's verdict.

The second, and even more memorable interview, was that with Professor Goldwin Smith, the former Oxford don whose eminence as a scholar and journalist had made him, in his old age, a kind of oracle whose words were listened to with respect even by those who differed violently with his views on Canada's political future.

At 83, Goldwin Smith was a lonely recluse among his books and memories in the fine old house, "The Grange," which he was to bequeath to Toronto as the nucleus of a civic art gallery. He had become unfriendly to newspaper reporters, having been frequently misquoted. The Star, especially, was in his bad books, and city editor Campbell picked me, as an innocent novice, to beard the lion in his den.

The subject of the interview was to be the grant of $15,000 to Alma College, a Methodist school for girls, by the ratepayers of St. Thomas, an act which had drawn protests from the Baptists of Ontario. I was a Baptist, and Goldwin Smith was known to favour the Baptist principle of strict separation of church and state. The odds on getting a good story were in my favour.

After a brief wait, I was led into the study by the butler—Professor Smith's secretary was away—and there, behind his great rosewood table, sat the tall, thin old man, with his bald head and short white sideburns, the tired eyes conveying an impression of great loneliness. He greeted me with a faint smile, listened sympathetically as I told him it was my first important assignment, asked about my college days, and then, in response to my questions, and to make sure he would not be misquoted, took up his pen and wrote the following statement:

There is no doubt that the Baptists are acting in accordance with their principles in resisting the grant out of public funds as a bonus to a denominational college. I may add my own earnest convictions that the Baptist principle of entire separation of the Church from the State is the true one, that it was laid down by the Founder of Christianity, and that departure from it has been the source of the greatest calamities alike to church and state. It would seem to me that resistance to the tax would be justified just so far as might be necessary to mark that the payment was involuntary and not a compromise of principle.

It was current gossip in those days that Goldwin Smith was an atheist. That with his own hand he capitalized the words "Founder of Christianity," and that, as I later learned, he frequently attended the little Baptist church on Beverley Street, may answer those who dubbed him a skeptic.

The page in his own handwriting containing the foregoing statement is one of my most prized possessions.

# 13 ⫷⫷⫷

## Plumbers and Preachers

MY SALARY went up to $15 a week when, on graduation from McMaster in May, 1905, I became a full-fledged Toronto *Star* reporter.

The *Star* was then in its second home under the Atkinson regime, the remodelled North of Scotland Chambers at 20 King Street West. Additional land had been purchased at the rear and it was the publisher's boast that, with the "biggest single newspaper site in Canada, we expect to have room enough to grow up with the country."

Magazine stories and motion pictures have portrayed the typical big city daily's news room as a madhouse presided over by an editor who foams at the mouth, swears sulphureously at his reporters, and literally tears unsatisfactory copy to shreds before consigning it to the waste paper basket.

Many newspapermen have denied that there ever was such an editor. But *Star* graduates of the early days know better. I learned much of what I know about reporting from just such a man.

Colin C. Campbell was one of the greatest city editors Canada has ever produced. He was on the *Star's* city desk when I first came there in 1904, a post he held for nearly twenty-four years. Always the first down in the morning, he was at his post until the last edition was on the press. Then he was off to the nearest barroom.

But no matter what transpired that night, he was back on the job at 7 a.m., clear-eyed, alert, and ready to direct his staff in a complete coverage of the day's news. And he expected the rest of us to be there too, just as promptly and just as alert.

The city editor of a metropolitan daily has no easy job. He must keep on top of the news, think quickly, and plan a day's work for each of his staff of fifteen to fifty men and women. And he must keep

tab on them all day long, arrange for their copy to reach his desk
with a minimum of delay, assess their stories, and indicate the space
to be given each and the type of heading wanted. Back in 1905 on
the *Star*, the city editor also superintended the make-up of the pages
when the type was set.

But despite these heavy responsibilities, Colin Campbell's roar
was always worse than his bite. He had a picturesque, expressive and
explosive vocabulary. Poor stories were torn up in your face and you
were told to write a better one or "get to hell out of here and stay
out." He could sense at once whether a reporter had really tried to
get the facts or was trying to put something over him. Only those
who were determined, come what may, to be newspapermen, could
take it; most others quit.

A veteran journalist who served under C. C. Campbell once
wrote of him: "The balloon ascends every day. Cub reporters think
he ought to be shut up in an iron cage through the bars of which
he could be fed with copy, instead of rambling around loose, tearing
paper into a thousand shreds."

But while he did tear up some stories, mine included, the same
"C. C. C." would, if he were not too rushed, take the trouble to reorganize a manuscript for a reporter with promise, and show him
where he had gone wrong.

Only in the hour before press deadline was he in a really savage
mood. Once the paper had been put to bed, Campbell turned human,
ribbing the very reporters whom, a few minutes earlier, he had been
cursing.

A native of Forestville, New York, he had been a police reporter
with the Hamilton *Spectator* before joining the staff of the Toronto
*News*. When on November 3, 1892, a group of labour men, locked
out of the *News*, founded the Toronto *Star*, Colin C. Campbell left
the former's city editorship to take on a like responsibility for its
newborn and not too promising rival. Without his genius and never-
say-die spirit it is highly unlikely the babe would have survived.

Time came when I was Campbell's assistant. When he was away
and I had to take over his duties, I was limp with exhaustion by early
afternoon. The tremendous quantity of copy which passed through
his hands in a single day still amazes me. He did as much as four or
five men do now.

How he managed to survive for a quarter century the rigours of
the city desk was one of the minor miracles of the Toronto *Star*.

Finally his health broke and he was retired on a small pension. But instead of dying as many expected, he listened to his wife, a Christian Science reader, embraced her religion, quit the bottle, and lived bright and cheery to the age of 85.

City editor Campbell gave his new recruit from McMaster University plenty to do that summer of 1905. And fortune smiled when one day he handed me a small clipping from a Toronto morning paper which reported a strike called in the shops of three Toronto plumbers. Strikes were not common occurrences then and he suggested an interview with the proprietors to find out what had happened.

One of the plumbers was eager to talk. He was sorer than the sorest of Job's boils and he spilled a story so hot that the other Toronto dailies were afraid to touch it for two days. From the three dissentient plumbers, and from labour organizers who had refused to comply with their bosses' request, we uncovered a scandal which rocked Toronto on its respectable heels.

The Master Plumbers' and Steamfitters' Co-operative Association, embracing most of the leading plumbing and heating firms in Toronto, set out to control by combine all lucrative jobs in the metropolitan area. A Central Supply Association, Ltd. bought and controlled all supplies. An agreement was reached with the labour union concerned that no union men would work for bosses not in the Co-operative Association.

To the secretary of the Co-operative, W. H. Meredith, the plumbers reported all contracts on which they were asked to tender. Three days later the various tenderers met, allocated the job among them, providing, through the exchange of IOU's ranging from $10 to $150, a share of the profit on the job to each "unsuccessful" tenderer, and including in the successful bid five per cent. for the benefit of Association office expenses.

Crown Attorney J. W. Curry ordered the police to raid the Association offices and the records were seized before they could be burned. Arraigned in court, the Master Plumbers' and Steamfitters' Co-operative Association and the Central Supply Association were found guilty on two counts and assessed fines totalling $10,000 each. Individual members were fined from $50 to $500, following assurance that their customers would be reimbursed.

I had been summoned as a Crown witness but fortunately Crown Attorney Curry was able to get all the evidence he needed from the Association's own books.

In passing judgment, Mr. Justice Clute bitterly denounced the business men before him, some of whom were prominent in city churches and stood high in Toronto's social circles. The *Star* carried full reports of all the proceedings. I learned early that J. E. Atkinson would never pull his punches to protect "big business."

Sin of a different sort made the headlines for me a second time in my first year on the *Star*. The winter of 1906 saw Toronto gripped by the most remarkable religious revival in half a century.

The city was literally turned upside down by the Rev. Dr. R. A. Torrey and Charles M. Alexander, two American evangelists fresh from an astonishing revival tour of Great Britain.

Scores of thousands attended their meetings; nearly 5,000 professed conversion; and churches were galvanized into new life, some of them not too willingly. In street cars, clubs, restaurants, and homes, the Torrey-Alexander meetings were the talk of the day.

City editor Campbell, knowing my interest in things religious, turned me loose on the story and gave me free rein. For thirty-one days, Sundays included, I worked from twelve to fifteen hours daily. Often I was up till near daybreak and more than once my reports covered a full eight-column page.

Massey Hall proved too small to hold the crowds, and overflow meetings, led by Crossley and Hunter, famous Canadian Methodists, were held in the nearby Metropolitan Church. Evangelists had come from all over the continent to help, and four hundred Ontario clergymen gathered in Toronto to hear an inspirational address by Torrey. The meetings were full of human interest, and people everywhere could be heard discussing them, pro and con, and humming or whistling the lilting hymn tunes with which they had become identified.

Torrey, a stern-faced man of middle age with white hair and vandyke beard, preached with sincerity and fervour, appealing to reason rather than emotion. Alexander, on the other hand, was a cheerful, unconventional man with a Tennessee accent and a fine tenor voice. Never had Toronto heard such congregational singing as that which he inspired. Shocked at first by his brisk, informal manner, Canadians were soon won over by his sunny smile and his warm friendliness. When he was teaching them to sing a new hymn, he would stop the music and ask cheerily, "Do you like it?" "Yes!" would come the answer in a great shout. "Then we'll have some more." And in a few minutes he would have the great crowd pouring out a volume of sound that fairly shook the rafters. He introduced the famous "Glory Song" of the Welsh revival to Canada:

O that will be . . . glory for me,
Glory for me . . . glory for me,
When by His grace I shall look on His face,
That will be glory . . . be glory for me.

He revived many of the old camp meeting hymns, like "The Old Time Religion," and among the most popular of his solos was the one whose refrain, "Tell Mother I'll Be There," provided a fine vehicle for massed voices.

During the meetings, volunteer workers moved about the hall, encouraging those who felt the call to a Christian life to make a public profession of faith. One of the volunteers approached the late Mel Hammond, who was covering the meetings for the Toronto *Globe*, then known as the Scotsman's Bible, and asked him if he had made his peace with God. "Oh, I'm a *Globe* reporter," answered Mel as if that settled it.

The two evangelists were greatly pleased with the *Star's* coverage of their meetings. Two years later when they separated, and Alexander formed a partnership with Rev. Dr. J. Wilbur Chapman for an evangelistic world-tour, I received a telegram from the latter offering me the post of publicity man at a salary considerably higher than I was getting from the *Star*. It was an opportunity to see the world, and the work would be interesting and useful. However, I was looking forward to getting married and chose the greater adventure at home.

# 14 ⫷⫷⫷

## Mill Boy to Millionaire

"I WOULD LIKE to have you as my secretary, Cranston, if you are willing," said publisher Atkinson one day in February, 1906, after he had congratulated me on my coverage of the Torrey-Alexander evangelistic meetings.

"It will give you a fine opportunity to see the paper from the inside and get an understanding of the business end of things. You need not stay longer than a year unless you wish," he added.

I accepted his offer. Often afterwards I regretted my decision to trade so soon the adventure of reporting for the desk end of journalism, but at the time it seemed like a step up the ladder.

Timothy Eaton had taught J. E. Atkinson his secret of business success. The *Star's* publisher was a guest at the Eaton summer home one weekend. On Sunday a slip of paper was handed to the founder of Canada's largest departmental store. Before slipping it into his pocket, Eaton said to his guest: "Have you any idea what was on that paper, Atkinson?"

"No, I have not," was the reply.

"That's what the boys took in on Saturday."

"I don't quite understand," said the *Star* publisher.

"It's what the boys at the store took in yesterday. Do you know what the *Star* took in Saturday?"

"I do not," Atkinson confessed.

"Then you should," Eaton replied.

Back in his office the following morning, J. E. Atkinson was soon getting daily reports on all aspects of his business.

One more lesson the *Star's* publisher learned from the same source. At a time when departmental stores were under severe attack, Atkinson asked Timothy Eaton: "What do you intend doing about it?"

"I'm going to keep store," was the answer.

Some years later, publisher Atkinson, keeping a sharp eye on his publishing costs, raised substantially Eaton's advertising rates. Timothy Eaton refused to sign a new contract and, for a full year, there was no Eaton advertising in the *Star* with a resultant big loss to both enterprises. Finally, however, Eatons came back in—and at Atkinson's price.

John Ross Robertson, founder and publisher of the Toronto *Telegram,* and J. E. Atkinson had no love for each other. Not only were they business rivals but their personalities differed markedly. Robertson insisted that the *Star's* slogan, "A Newspaper Not an Organ," should read "An Organ Not a Newspaper," as its news was coloured to suit the views of its publisher. And Atkinson could say the same with some force of the *Telegram.*

In the early days when they met on the street it was customary for Robertson to greet his rival with, "Well, Joe, is it paying yet?"

For some years the honest response was, "No, it is not."

Then one day Atkinson countered with, "Yes, it paid last month."

"Just a fluke," growled the *Telegram* publisher. "You will never make it go." And again he advised the *Star's* president to give up the fight and join the staff of one of the well established papers.

But soon after that the "yes" reply to Robertson's standard question became so frequent that he quit asking. The fun of embarrassing Atkinson had gone forever.

Every day the business office sent to the *Star* publisher a complete record of all advertising earnings for the previous twenty-four hours. He knew how much money had come in from the east side of the city, the west side, from national accounts, and from classified advertisers. On each statement was recorded the earnings of the same day last year. When the trend was down, a note from the chief followed quickly.

As his secretary, I added figures, divided them, multiplied and subtracted till I was dizzy. My chief was always wanting to know the costs of some new aspect of his business, and he would take time to explain fully his purposes. I learned early that the great secret of financial success is to watch the pennies. But Joseph Atkinson had had an even earlier introduction to this lesson.

If he had a hardness which did not always seem to fit his editorial professions, it was because he came up the hard way. If he was sometimes parsimonious, it was because he counted his first earnings in pennies not dollars. His was a struggle from poverty to extreme wealth and, like many others who travelled the same road, he was a compound of contradictions.

His father, Joseph Atkinson, who operated a mill two miles from the village of Newcastle, Ontario, was killed one night by a train while walking home along the tracks. Joseph Junior, the youngest of a family of five boys and three girls, was but six months old at the time.

Widowed Hannah Atkinson moved her big brood into Newcastle, and supported them by taking in boarders from a nearby woollen mill.

The Atkinson home had an atmosphere of devout Methodism. There were but two books, the Bible and the Methodist hymnal. The dominant and controlling interest in Joseph's life was religion, and the dinner table discussions of the mill workers' grievances gave that religion a social emphasis. Ever afterwards J. E. Atkinson had a deep sympathy for the Christian ministry. No other Canadian newspaper had as many clergymen on its staff or as contributors as did the Toronto *Star*.

At school he did well, but did not excel, hampered by a block stammer which, under stress, made him speechless. About two incidents of his school days he spoke on several occasions. A new teacher, a two-fisted red-head, was placed in charge of the one room school. The first morning Joseph Atkinson was asked to read aloud. He got to his feet but could make not a sound. Interpreting silence as disobedience, the new master started to thrash him. Immediately the other youngsters rushed to Joseph's defence, grabbed the teacher's arm and explained about the stammer. The teacher apologized publicly and he and Atkinson for sixty years remained fast friends. That incident, J. E. Atkinson used to say, taught him two of the basic principles of journalism: first, be sure of your facts; and second, never be ashamed to admit a mistake.

The other incident which lived in his memory happened when he was eight years old. He was sitting one evening by the frozen surface of a small Newcastle pond, watching the other children skate. Suddenly there appeared beside him a fashionably-dressed young woman. She asked why he was not skating with the other children.

"Because I have no skates yet," Joseph replied, without envy.

Whereupon she took him by the hand to the village store, bought skates, helped him put them on, and informed him they were his for keeps. His brothers grabbed young Joseph by the arms and dragged him in a circle around the ice. When he looked again for his benefactress, she was gone. He never saw her again. But all through his life, he referred to her as "Lady Luck," and declared she had led him by the hand many, many times.

When Joseph was fourteen, his mother died, worn out. He left school and worked as piecer boy in the local woollen mill until its destruction by fire deprived him of a job. For a while he attended Newcastle high school and then found work at $8 a month in the local post office. This included supplying weekly news from Newcastle for the Port Hope *Times*. He had to wait three years for a raise to $9 a month.

His newspaper career began when J. D. Trayes, publisher of the Port Hope *Times*, hired him at $6 a week to collect accounts in and around Port Hope. The young man proved a hard worker, and was soon bringing in new subscriptions and looking after news items and printing jobs. When, a year later, the *Times* became a daily, Joseph Atkinson, now 20, was chief reporter and in charge of the editorial page at $9 a week. During Trayes' frequent long absences, he was responsible for getting out the paper and steering the business through its recurrent financial difficulties. But when the mortgagees asked him to take over the paper, he refused out of loyalty to the man who had given him his start. In later years, J. E. Atkinson was offered two other papers—the Stratford *Beacon-Herald* and the Chatham *Planet*—if he would assume their mortgages and debts. Both he refused.

It was in Port Hope that Joseph Atkinson was introduced to books. His employer had a large and well assorted library, and Atkinson delved into many fields of knowledge and became familiar with great authors. Indeed it was in this library his ultimate career took shape. One day Trayes suggested that his young editor should read Charles Dent's *Fathers of Confederation*. One sentence in that book changed his whole mental outlook. He read that Sir Leonard Tilley had "risen from a drug store clerk to be a statesman." If Tilley could do it, why not Atkinson? It was from then on, my chief said, that he began to read with purpose—biographies, social studies, philosophy, history.

After four years with the *Times,* his employer having refused to increase his pay, young Atkinson saw an advertisement for a reporter in the Toronto *World.* He applied, and in October, 1888, was hired at $15 a week. One of his first jobs was to write a column and a half of editorials, and soon he was doing this regularly.

Atkinson had been with the *World* only four months when Sir John Willison, editor of the *Globe,* hired him away at two dollars more a week to cover the Ontario Legislature, with the promise of later being sent to the press gallery at Ottawa.

The young man put all his energies into his work. He neither smoked nor drank and was little interested in social pursuits. He attended the Methodist church regularly, and spent his spare time reading books on economics and politics. He was strongly affected at this time by Henry George's *Progress and Poverty,* and became in principles and politics a confirmed liberal.

In 1891 he received the coveted assignment to the Commons Press Gallery, and remained Ottawa correspondent of the *Globe* during six sessions. There he met Wilfrid Laurier, rising hope of the Liberal party. Between sessions he was given other important assignments in various parts of Canada, meeting the leaders in all phases of Canada's development as the *Globe's* chief reporter.

Seven years later he was offered and accepted the post of managing editor of the Montreal *Herald,* another Liberal newspaper. His work there attracted the notice of Sir Hugh Graham, who invited him to become managing editor of his powerful Montreal *Star.* It was a tempting offer, second in importance among newspaper jobs in Canada. But the *Star* was Conservative in politics, and Atkinson hesitated. He consulted Willison of the *Globe,* who advised him to take it. Still Atkinson hung back.

Then Willison recalled that a group of Toronto Liberals were planning to buy a little evening paper, the Toronto *Star,* which had been leading a precarious existence since its launching seven years before by some striking printers with the aim of strengthening trade unionism in that city. Willison recommended that the prospective buyers engage Atkinson as publisher.

Atkinson faced a difficult three-way choice: to remain in his comfortable job on the growing *Herald;* to become managing editor of the wealthy and powerful Montreal *Star;* or to become publisher of a despised and moribund four-page newspaper in a city already over-supplied with newspapers—the *Globe, Mail and Empire,* and *World* in the morning field, and the Evening *Globe,* the *Telegram,* the *News* and the *Star* in the afternoon. But his spirit rose to the challenge. He chose the risk and struggle—and opportunity—presented by the Toronto paper.

In a meeting with Senator Cox, Walter Massey and the Hon. Lyman Jones, the terms were agreed upon. Atkinson insisted that the *Star* should be conducted solely in its own interests as a newspaper enterprise. There must be no interference from outside, and no attempt to control it in the interests of any party or group. Secondly, Atkinson stipulated that he should have the right to buy in treasury stock, and the first option on any stock of which the purchaser might wish to dispose at any time.

The idea of "no interference" was new to Senator Cox, and he suggested that Atkinson consult Mr. Laurier. Laurier asked Atkinson who would decide what was in the best interests of the paper. "I would have to do that," replied Atkinson. "That is the only way a newspaper could be successfully conducted," admitted the Liberal chief.

The deal was closed, and on December 13, 1899, J. E. Atkinson became publisher of the Toronto *Daily Star.*

Purchase price was $32,000. The company was capitalized at $100,000, of which $25,000 was held in the treasury, the balance being subscribed by ten Liberals. Atkinson was to receive an annual salary of $5,000—$3,000 in cash and the rest in stock. This would give him, at the end of five years, a holding of $10,000, equal to that of any other shareholder. In 1905, when the paper was moved to new offices on King Street, the capital was raised to $200,000.

Atkinson once told me that he and his wife undertook to live on half his cash salary, and with the other half to buy stock. This meant frugal living for a time. But by this arrangement, and by borrowing money to buy in stock as it became available, within seven years he owned $102,000 worth, or 51 per cent. of the *Star's* stock.

At the outset, he received a rude shock. The purchasers had been told the *Star's* circulation was 14,000. It proved to be only 7,000. Atkinson ordered the advertising department to make no more false claims. Within a year, however, the circulation was up to 9,888. By

1902 it was 14,000 and by 1904, when I joined the staff for the summer, it had risen to 31,000.

The acumen and industry of the mill boy who had been forced to work hard and save pennies, who had grown up in a deeply religious household, had experienced at first hand the problems of the wage-earner, and acquired his social philosophy from Henry George and such liberal thinkers as Wilfrid Laurier, had proven that a newspaper which combined shrewd business management with a popular appeal and humanitarian sympathies could be made a success in Tory Toronto against what seemed overwhelming odds.

# 15 ⋘

## Back to the City Room

AFTER A YEAR as his secretary, in which he had become fully acquainted with my limitations as stenographer, typist, and mathematician, Atkinson said to me one day: "I think it is perhaps about time you went back to the editorial department. You have learned a lot here that will be useful to you."

I heartily concurred in his suggestion and found soon thereafter that I had been named assistant city editor of the *Star*.

One of my first assignments was to interview Admiral Robert E. Peary who was about to set out on the final Arctic journey which took him to the North Pole. He talked freely of his plans and dreams. I will never forget that strong, tall, loosely-built man with far-seeing eyes who said to me quietly as we parted: "I shall make it this time." Unfortunately most of the glory that should have been his was temporarily stolen by the false claims of that bold faker Dr. Frederick Cook who claimed to have beaten Peary to the earth's top.

That summer we introduced the *Star's* first sporting extra. I sat by the telegraph ticker and, as the score of each baseball inning and racing news came in, ran to the pressroom where the presses were stopped long enough to permit the latest results to be hammered with a punch on to the plates. These sports editions materially boosted our street sales.

In the fall of 1907 I was given a job I had coveted since first there was ink on my fingers—parliamentary correspondent in the press gallery at Ottawa.

When I arrived at the Capital, however, I was surprised and no little disturbed at the cool reception accorded the *Star*. The other members of the Gallery resented the light way in which my paper treated Canada's parliament. No *Star* man was ever there long, and the House of Commons debates were not reported unless they were unusually colourful. The *Globe* and the *Mail and Empire,* as Toronto morning papers, provided coverage of the House a half a day before the *Star* could hope to, so my work was largely done outside the Commons, digging up Departmental stories and answering queries sent me by Managing Editor Bone. Then, as always, the *Star* was much more interested, as were its readers, in the human interest side of the Ottawa news than in attempting to present a full interpretation of national legislation.

However, the coolness gradually abated, and some of the old-timers became friendly and helpful. Another newcomer with whom I formed a firm friendship was Fred Landon of the London *Free Press,* later professor of history and librarian at the University of Western Ontario, and finally its Vice-President. Our friendship continued through the years, and latterly found an additional bond in our common interest in the archaeological excavations at old Fort Ste. Marie near Midland.

The debates in the House fascinated me. Sir Wilfrid Laurier was in his best fighting form, and when word spread that the Old Man was on his feet the seats on both sides of the House filled rapidly. Rising to the full height of his slim, graceful figure, with the famous "white plume" giving him the air of a knight entering the lists, he would stir his followers to applause with skilful rapier thrusts at the Opposition, or hold the entire House spellbound with his eloquence. For all his mastery of the English tongue, he was tireless in his quest for the precise word or phrase. In dull moments in the House he would send for a large Webster's dictionary, which he would study with seeming absorption, but always with a keen ear attuned to what was going on.

Hon. Rodolphe Lemieux, whose English had less of a French accent than Laurier's, was another eloquent speaker and with great ability to appeal to the emotions. Hon. George Foster, whose analytical mind was thoroughly at home in the realm of public finance; Hon. W. S. Fielding, quick-witted and sharp-tongued; Hon. George P. Graham, publisher of the Brockville *Recorder,* who could always be depended upon for a laugh when proceedings grew dull (as frequently happened when Hon. R. L. Borden, leader of the Opposition, had the floor); Hon. Frank Oliver, the blunt publisher of the Edmonton *Bulletin,* with his handle-bar mustache—these were some of the outstanding figures in the House at that time. Among the back benchers were William Lyon Mackenzie King, the former Toronto newspaper reporter, and W. F. "Billy" Maclean, publisher of the Toronto *World*, a newspaper whose shaky financial position often compelled its owner's absence from the House.

My fate was that of my *Star* predecessors. I was at Ottawa little more than three months, being recalled before the session's end. I had filed plenty of copy from both the House and the Departments, but little of it had been used. Chorus girls are always more newsworthy than politicians—except when the two get mixed up together —and I was at Ottawa at the time of the trial of Harry K. Thaw, New York millionaire playboy, who shot Stamford White, wealthy architect, for becoming too friendly with his chorus girl wife Evelyn. The court hearings were a colossal crime sensation. The *Star* published endless columns of stenographic reports of the proceedings of the sordid bedroom drama. Then followed immediately the crash of the Sovereign and Ontario Banks. No matter what I might have uncovered at Ottawa it would have had unbeatable competition.

Despite my failure to supply sufficiently colourful news from the Capital, I was rewarded with a trip south. I was assigned to cover the Toronto baseball club on its spring training jaunt through the Tri-State League. Those were the days when big, blond, good-natured "Mike" Kelley was the manager, and the stars were "Dick" Rudolph, who later made the New York Giants, and Fred Mitchell whose hurling earned him a berth with the Boston Braves. The only Canadian on the team was second baseman Jimmy Cockman who had learned some of his baseball in my home town of Galt.

But despite the interesting routine of morning practices, afternoon exhibition games, and the swing through the towns and cities of the Pennsylvania coal country, my most vivid memory is that of the day in Reading, Pa. when I was shocked to see a Toronto player come into the hotel followed by a tall, very thin, shabbily dressed woman, her face sad and lined with care. As she entered, she looked back tenderly to a little girl seated on a nearby park bench, waiting. The man and woman went through the hall to his bedroom. Prostitutes, of course, seek customers wherever they can find them, and ball players are fair game. But I hated that man and I was glad when he failed to make the team.

"Lol" Solman owned the Toronto Ball Club at that time as well as operating the Royal Alexandra Theatre in the same city. A wealthy man, he was constantly launching new enterprises, and Torontonians thought themselves lucky to get in on the ground floor with Solman. When he bought Fairweather's Store on lower Yonge Street, and refitted it as Prince's Restaurant with a New York manager, it looked like a gold mine and I put $500 of my savings into its stock. This time, however, Solman wasn't lucky and the enterprise, loaded with terrific expenses, went bankrupt. He need not, of course, have been concerned about the loss suffered by a young newspaperman but one day he sent for me and said: "I know you put your money into this business because you had faith in my ability. Please do not tell any-one what I am going to do, but I want you to accept an equivalent amount in common shares of Loew's London Theatre. They have no great value at present but I am sure they will come." Two years later I was able to sell those shares for $300. Solman has been dead for many years, but I will always remember his uncalled-for generosity.

Charity in a somewhat different form was to occupy much of my time for the next two years. The Star Santa Claus Fund had been launched only the year before with George Maitland, present editor of the *Star,* in charge. That fund and the Star Fresh Air Fund were now entrusted to me.

Through these charitable projects many thousands of children were made happy—and the *Star* profited from the goodwill engendered among its readers. It was Atkinson's good fortune to combine public charity with private advantage.

My work included the writing of appeals for money, to which the paper gave generous space and, in the case of the Santa Claus Fund, the arrangements for packing and distributing parcels. The Fresh Air Fund money was handled entirely by the Children's Aid Society, the Neighborhood Workers' Association, and other church and charitable organizations which also supplied the names for the Santa Claus distribution.

For the first year the Santa Claus parcels were packed in the Sunday School hall of Trinity Anglican Church in the east end of the city, whose beloved rector, Canon H. C. Dixon, was an indefatig-able worker amongst the poor of that district. The next year volunteer workers, some of them from the *Star's* staff, looked after the packing and distributing, using a rented warehouse as headquarters. Both years, my wife and I, with the aid of a few friends, handled the job of filling paper bags with biscuits donated by a Toronto firm. Donations of toys, clothing and other articles by the department stores and various manufacturers helped to swell the packages.

Another of my responsibilities during this period was "Everybody's Column," in which readers' questions were answered. I used encyclopedias, dictionaries and all sorts of reference books to inform our readers on almost every branch of human knowledge and experience, from love to law, from etiquette to theology, from health to household management. Sometimes, on legal or medical matters, a lawyer or doctor was paid a fee to provide authentic information or advice.

I also organized a new filing system for newspaper cuts, and a library file in which photographs and clippings were preserved and indexed. These two files formed the nucleus of a "morgue" which my successor, Jerry Elder, a man of indomitable energy and industry and with a genius for organization, developed on a much more extensive scale. Elder was succeeded by the Rev. A. F. "Biddy" Barr of Toronto Varsity football fame, under whose direction the *Star* library became the finest and most complete to be found on any Canadian newspaper, and was ultimately thrown open for the use of the general public.

Under my direction, also, a syndicate department was organized to sell *Star* feature articles and photographs to other Canadian newspapers.

As a sort of general utility man, who also filled in for the city editor when he was ill or away, I was given by managing editor John R. Bone the title of assistant managing editor.

For some years, Atkinson had been his own managing editor. But, as the *Star* grew, and business details absorbed more of his time, he looked about for a man to take over his post.

The natural choice would have been Colin C. Campbell, the dynamic city editor who had made the *Star's* news columns the liveliest in the city. Mr. Atkinson urged him to delegate some of his duties and free himself for greater responsibility. But "C. C. C." could not bring himself to give up copy handling. So Atkinson selected as his helper John R. Bone, a reporter of outstanding ability, and in 1907 gave him his own post of managing editor.

For the next twenty-one years, John Bone occupied a position second in importance only to President Atkinson's. While Bone was prepared to give prominence to human interest stories, he did not believe in making the *Star* primarily a purveyor of sensationalism. It was all right to devote space to the Thaw murder trial, but he was anxious that the *Star* would also win a reputation for solid and accurate news coverage, attracting readers who sought information rather than entertainment.

Son of a Scottish pioneer farmer, John Bone received his early education in a little red school house in Huron County, at Clinton high school and London Collegiate Institute. In 1899 he graduated from the University of Toronto with first class honours in mathematics. His logical mind and his mathematical training were reflected in the sound thinking and clarity of expression that characterized his articles. An exceptionally retentive memory enabled him to report speeches and interviews without taking notes.

These qualities were conspicuously displayed in a number of important activities.  He conducted many of the negotiations with trade unions. He became a director of the Canadian Associated Press and Canadian Press Ltd., and played an influential part in making these news-distributing agencies independent of British subsidies. He was one of the first Canadian directors of the North American Newspaper Alliance, an international news and feature syndicate. He served successively as secretary-treasurer, vice-president and president of the Canadian Press Association, then a fraternal organization of newspaper and magazine publishers. He was also president at one time of The University Club, the Toronto Canadian Club, the University College Literary Society, and the University of Toronto lacrosse club.

John Bone was a man of keen mind and progressive temperament. He was conscientious and painstaking in his work, modest and reserved in manner, and kindly and companionable in his relations with others. He moved easily in the city's intellectual and financial circles, and had a host of friends and admirers. He was, above all, a family man who found great joy in his home.

But despite the importance of his work in the *Star's* rise to success and fortune, John Bone remained solely an employee. He was given enough stock to enable him to vote at *Star* business meetings but with the firm understanding that it was to be returned on demand.

And in the early years, despite his post as managing editor, he apparently found it necessary to make some money on the side. He received the "Chief's" permission to act as Canadian correspondent for a group of British and American newspapers. Atkinson may have believed it would be of value to have his managing editor make such connections. At any rate, he encouraged it, and saved money for the *Star*.

John Bone sent a weekly letter to six foreign periodicals. Material for the letter was gathered from articles appearing in the *Daily Star* and other Canadian publications. Many of these articles were written by *Star* men to the managing editor's orders and first appeared in the *Star*. Then Bone's stenographer typed them out, altering a word here and there, and sent them abroad over his signature. This practice puzzled the *Star's* top reporters. They did not enjoy seeing digests of their own articles appearing in other papers under Bone's name even though they had been paid for their work. It was just as legitimate as it is for a retailer to buy goods from one man and sell them as his own to another. But somehow it seemed a little different when one dealt in words and ideas.

For more than two years before John Bone's death, in addition to the heavy burden of directing the daily publication of a large newspaper, he spent hours, day and night, planning the details of the *Star's* new skyscraper home. A threatened printers' strike added to his worries. When he died suddenly on June 7, 1928, following a severe heart attack, I felt he had sacrificed his life in the devotion he gave to the *Star's* advancement.

I got along well with John Bone. He gave me his confidence when he made me his assistant and charged me with carrying out his ideas.

In those years *Star* men were active in the Canadian Press Association. J. E. Atkinson had held successively the posts of assistant secretary-treasurer and secretary-treasurer. Now John Bone was in the latter job and J. T. Clark, editor of the *Star*, on the Association executive. Bone encouraged me to join the Canadian Press in 1908— the year David Williams of the Collingwood *Bulletin* was president— and the next year asked me to be his assistant. When he was elected second vice-president in 1910, I became secretary-treasurer, holding that office for two years.

The Canadian Press Association was then a great journalistic fraternity, open to all who worked on newspapers, daily or weekly, as well as on magazines or other periodicals. Founded in 1859, it had done much to foster understanding and goodwill between all parts of Canada. William Gillespy, editor of the Hamilton *Spectator*, was its founder and first president.

Its principal aim was social and fraternal. Members came from coast to coast to discuss mutual interests and problems, but mainly for the purpose of social intercourse. An excursion to some place of interest in Canada was a feature of the annual programme. I recall visits to the Porcupine goldfields, to Quebec City and to Regina. The newspapermen were always handsomely entertained.

John M. Imrie was the man who brought new ideas to the Canadian Press Association. Then editor of Canadian *Printer and Publisher,* he astonished the members by declaring that most of them did not know whether they were making or losing money. Under his stimulus, publishers began installing cost accounting systems. They became really money conscious for the first time.

This was particularly true of the daily newspaper publishers. They broke away and formed their own Canadian Daily Newspapers Association, gradually abandoning the social objectives of the Association's founders. Imrie became secretary-treasurer, then manager, of the daily group. The weekly publishers formed their own association, whose objects continued to be mainly fraternal. My heart was with the weeklies, but being then on the staff of the *Daily Star* I went with the CDNA.

After some years, Imrie joined the Southam organization as business manager of the Hamilton *Spectator.* In 1921 he went west to become managing director of the Edmonton *Journal,* and later its vice-president. An able and straightforward man, he was the soul of honour and uprightness. He became a power in the newspaper business in Alberta, and when that province had a case to present at Ottawa, John Imrie was usually asked to present it.

When I acquired the Midland *Free Press* in 1935, I joined the Canadian Weekly Newspapers Association, and once more enjoyed the fellowship of men in the same business. Some of them were old friends like C. Harold Hale of the Orillia *Packet and Times,* J. Alex MacLaren of the Barrie *Examiner,* and David Williams of the Collingwood *Enterprise-Bulletin,* all fellow publishers in Simcoe County. Another was a still older friend, the late Arthur Wright, publisher of the Mount Forest *Confederate,* who had many years before tried to teach me French at the Galt Collegiate Institute.

# 16 «««

## *They Died in Harness*

THE RAPID GROWTH of the *Star* in its early years was the product of the genius of more than one man. Around J. E. Atkinson, in addition to John Bone, was a group of faithful, hard-working, and conscientious executives who gave their best in his service. And it was no small best.

One of the greatest of these newspaper men was W. L. "Bill" Argue, the *Star's* circulation manager. Recognized by his fellow circulation managers of Canada and the United States as the dean of their profession, he was elected in 1920 president of their International Association and later made a life member.

Bill Argue's first job was on a farm near Oshawa but in 1885 he moved to Toronto to work as a salesman in Eaton's shoe department. Two years later he joined the circulation staff of the Toronto *News* as a canvasser in the city's Christie pits district. There were then six Toronto dailies—the *Globe* and the *Mail,* each of which published both morning and evening editions; the *Empire* and the *World,* morning papers; and the *Evening Telegram* and the evening *News.* It was in 1894, just two years after the *Star* had been launched by printers locked out by the *News,* that Bill Argue joined the circulation department of the city's newest and smallest daily. Its circulation was then 7,000. When he died, 45 years later, it had grown to 220,000.

Despite his driving energy in the sale of newspapers, Argue was a quiet, somewhat retiring man, with a fine sense of humour and an ever present desire to talk about the old days when it was anybody's guess whether the *Star* would live or die. In its early years the *Star* distributed its papers throughout the city by two-wheel horse-drawn carts which cost its publisher $25 per week. Argue lived to see the day when the *Star's* motor transport fleet was one of the largest, fastest, and most efficient of any industry on the continent, delivering papers daily to all parts of southern Ontario. He had, as a youth, an excellent training for this province-wide transportation network. As an enthusiastic member of the Queen City Bicycle Club he had pedalled over many hundreds of miles of Ontario's highways and byways, then unpaved.

Bill Argue stayed at his post until within two weeks of his death on May 24, 1939, at the age of 75. He should have been retired years before on a well-earned and generous pension. He told me he had mentioned the matter several times to Atkinson only to be told that it was under consideration. However in a friendly letter written by the *Star's* president a few days after the death of his circulation manager, were these words in his own handwriting:

"Mr. Argue wanted to 'die in harness' and declined pensioning. He and his wife and doctor agreed that it was best for him to come to the office for a couple of hours per day at least." Many an older man, when he faces up to the stark reality of enforced idleness, backs away from it.

When this great circulation man passed on, he was acclaimed for his ability, integrity, genuineness, decency and kindliness. There was not one among us who did not feel the poorer. He was truly one of God's gentlemen.

Another one of the members of the former Toronto *News* staff inherited by Atkinson when he took over as publisher of the *Star* was Walter C. R. Harris. With a boy and two women, one of whom combined the duties of bookkeeper, secretary and cashier, he constituted the *Star's* complete business office staff when the paper was launched.

A native of the Channel Islands, Harris came to Toronto as a child and was well known as a lacrosse and football player as well as an excellent bowler and billiardist. Handsome in looks and character, he was able, diligent, kindly, and a man of considerable business sagacity. At one point he was successful in securing some of the *Star* stock which had unexpectedly come on the market. J. E. Atkinson was not pleased that Harris had beaten him to the buy. Walter refused all overtures from his chief to purchase the shares, and warned his wife not to sell them to anyone without first advertising them publicly. However, shortly after Harris' death at the age of 65 on February 24, 1934, the stock came into Atkinson's possession as had so many shares before.

# 17 «««

## Napoleons of the Sports Page

WHEN J. E. ATKINSON came to Toronto to take over the *Star*, he brought with him a young man who was to shine on its sports pages for the next thirty-one years.

Many famous Canadian newspaper men got their start delivering papers and one of the most notable was W. A. "Bill" Hewitt. Born in Cobourg, Ontario, he moved with his family to Toronto while still a youngster and there took on a paper route for the morning *Empire*. Fascinated by the world of journalism, he went down town each day after school to hold copy for proofreader Sam Mitchell in the office of the Toronto *News*. Young Hewitt scribbled small news items which were relayed to the city editor and occasionally printed.

One day while he was holding copy, the door opened and George Darby, the *News'* big and brusque business manager, boomed out:

"Boy, is your name Hewitt?"

"Yes-yes, sir," stammered little Bill, sure he had done something wrong, and would be fired.

"Do you want to be a reporter, boy?" came the big voice.

"Yes-yes, sir," answered Bill shakily.

"Then go home and tell your mother to get you a pair of long pants, and come down in the morning."

Although Bill was sixteen he was still in shorts.

Next morning in his first longs he was down at seven and never went back to school.

City editor Charlie Ryan, who was also news editor, wire editor, foreign editor and nearly every other editor, gave him some news paragraphs to re-write. Then he was sent out to report a funeral and later a wedding. That done, he was despatched to the Central

Prison where he saw a man, guilty of a sex offence, being given fifteen lashes.

"I was scared stiff," said Bill. "I could have got the story just as well if I had not gone in but I did not know that. So I went with Warden Gilmour to see the whipping, a horrible sight. That was my first day."

Like many city editors of the time, Ryan went out frequently to the "barber shop." One day Bill's name was left off the assignment book. Again he feared he was being fired. But when the other reporters had gone, Ryan asked Hewitt to sit at his desk while he went to the "barber shop." He was told to read whatever the reporters brought in, write headings, and place the edited copy on the hook.

"I was pretty scared," said Bill, "but did what I was told." Soon the composing room foreman came in and asked for Ryan. Told he was out, the foreman demanded: "What'll I do for copy?"

"There's some on the hook," said Bill.

"Who got it ready?"

"I did. Mr. Ryan told me to."

"Holy Jehoshaphat!" exclaimed the foreman. "A kid is getting the paper out."

Again and again this happened, and steadily Bill gained confidence. Then C. C. Campbell, later city editor of the *Star,* came on the *News* staff. Hewitt drifted to the sports department and eventually became sports editor.

It was while on reporting assignments that Bill Hewitt came to know Joe Atkinson, then a young scribe with the rival Toronto *Globe.* They got along well. When Atkinson went to Montreal as managing editor of the *Herald,* he invited Hewitt to go along. But Bill was just about to be married and he postponed acceptance for a year.

One day he received a wire from Montreal asking him to arrange an interview for Atkinson in Toronto with Senator Cox and other prominent Liberals. They were thinking of buying the *Star,* which was in difficulties. When Atkinson met Hewitt on his arrival in Toronto, he advised him to stay and await developments there. But Hewitt, hearing no more about it, went to Montreal and started with the *Herald.*

He had been there only a short time, however, when Atkinson took him aside and said:

"What would you think, Bill, if I made an offer for the Toronto *Star?*"

"You would be putting your head in a noose," replied Bill. "Toronto is a Tory city, and the *Star* is a Liberal paper."

"You are wrong," said J. E. Atkinson. "I have a slogan that will do the trick. 'A newspaper not an organ.' The *Star* will be an independent paper."

When Atkinson became publisher of the *Star,* young Hewitt went with him as his sports editor, a post he held until 1930. He then resigned to become manager of the Maple Leaf Gardens, but continued to write two columns, "Sporting News and Reviews," and "Topics of the Turf," for the *Star.* When he found it impractical to carry on both jobs, he gave up his *Star* connection.

The final break was undoubtedly hastened by the fact that Foster Hewitt, Bill's clever son, left the *Star* and went to the Gardens along with his father. Foster was interested in radio before most of us even dreamed of it. After working with the Independent Telephone Company in the days of crystal sets, he had joined the staff of the Toronto *Star's* new radio station CFCA first as an announcer and later as manager, succeeding Eddie Bowers. It was "Conn" Smythe who invited Foster Hewitt to take charge of the Maple Leaf Gardens radio programmes. Sensing a big opportunity, young Hewitt refused all overtures from the *Star,* though finally offered four times the salary he was then getting.

Bill Hewitt is one of the finest sportsmen and sports editors Canada has known. Never has there been the slightest scandal connected with his name. And in addition to his other duties, he has, for over fifty years, been the efficient and popular secretary of the Ontario Hockey Association, a truly remarkable record.

Lou Marsh, who succeeded Bill Hewitt as sports editor of the *Daily Star,* was another of the pioneers who antedated the Atkinson regime. Printers' ink had marked him early too. At the age of fourteen he was a *Star* copy boy in the old *Saturday Night* building on Adelaide Street. When he died March 5, 1936, from a cerebral hemorrhage, he had put in forty-three years of consecutive service.

Lou was a good athlete as well as a fine sports writer. Few games there were he could not play well. Big and strong in frame, he once was a lineman on the senior Argonaut rugby team. Fast on his feet, he was a creditable sprinter. He swam like a duck, loved to sail sloops and ice boats, drove sea fleas at high speed, could handle his fists well in the ring, and played a good game of baseball. Reckless, clever and carefree, he enjoyed life to the full.

Perhaps it was on the water that Lou got most fun. When the waves were rolling high, the winds bellying the sails taut, and the spray dashing in his face, he was happy. At least fifteen times he plunged into the icy waters of Lake Ontario to rescue drowning people. One Spring day at Toronto's eastern beaches, a young lad was being carried out to the open lake on an ice cake. Lou, disregarding his then serious heart condition, grabbed a rope and waded and swam through the freezing water until he was able to carry the kiddie to safety.

But it was as a hockey referee that Marsh became best known throughout the cities and towns of Ontario. Lou knew that the public liked action, and tried to make the players deliver.

Little places take their hockey seriously. When the home team loses, the referee is often blamed. On many occasions it was only Lou's quick wit that saved him from the angry fans.

"The only way to stop a mob rush is to go after the first man and down him with a fast wallop," said Lou. "If you bungle it you are in a bad way."

One night a burly heavyweight led a gang of hot-heads into the referee's dressing room. He made straight for Lou who still had his skates on. Jumping to his feet Marsh buried his head in the heavyweight's belly, and pushed him backwards until he sat on a red hot stove. With a howl of anguish the big chap ran for safety and Lou walked out unmolested.

Mobbed one night at Cannington, Lou told me he made his way to the train without much difficulty. "The men were easy to handle. They were all bundled up in overcoats, while I had only a sweater," said Lou. "Besides I had a big brass bell in one hand and a pair of sharp skates on my feet."

Lou Marsh was no slouch either when it came to general reporting. When the palatial steamship *Titanic* ran into an iceberg in the Atlantic and sank with a tragic loss of life, he was sent to New York with other *Star* reporters to meet the Toronto survivors at the pier and get their stories. With him went his friend Harry Rosenthal.

No one knew who had been saved, and the problem of discovering who aboard the rescue ship were Toronto people seemed insoluble.

Steamship officials and police were doing all they could to protect the nerve-wracked survivors from reporters.

Said Marsh to Rosenthal: "You stand up on that pile of ropes and yell 'I have messages for Toronto people. Toronto people this way, please'."

It worked. Lou stood on the ground level and greeted each Torontonian as he or she heeded the call. He got a dozen names and interviews, and scored a major scoop for the *Star*.

As a writer Lou had a style all his own. People little interested in sport read his "Pick and Shovel" column just for its vibrant freshness. If he was stumped for a word he invented one, and some of these have become a permanent part of the Canadian language. "Seaflea," as applied to those tiny high-powered motorcraft which skim at 40 miles or more per hour on the water's surface, is one.

Whimsical jokes were also in Lou's line. He had the whole city laughing for weeks with the strange creatures he created and placed in the *Star* window so that skeptics might see with their own eyes. One of these was the "wambeazle," an odd looking fish with the head of a horned rabbit, which, he wrote, was first cousin to the "whiffen-pooper" and the "whamgoofer." The only way it could be shot was behind a "schnozzlehound" who, just as soon as he spied a "wambeazle," would stand on his hind legs and dance a hula hula upside down. Then he whiffed his ears and wobbled his nose. The "wambeazle" laughed so hard that he could not run away, and was therefore easy to shoot.

Lou Marsh reported one day that he had been up to the Holland River marsh and caught a "whiffenfish." He threw a plug of tobacco into the water and grabbed the fish when it came up to spit. The "Whatisit," a petrified specimen of a pre-war mermaid or golliwog carp, also had its Marshian origin in the Holland River area. His "Shebe," a mummified Chinese man fish, was used by Lou to prove to the entertainment of his thousands of readers that the North American continent was once inhabited by Mongols. The sports page lacked neither colour nor humour when Lou was at its helm.

His name is now perpetuated by the *Star's* Lou Marsh Trophy, awarded annually to Canada's outstanding athlete of the year. It is a fitting memorial to a man who, time and time again, won in his readers' eyes the title of outstanding sports editor of the year, and who added circulation by the thousands to Canada's fastest growing daily newspaper.

# 18 ⋘

## *His Pictures Made History*

WHEN FIRST I JOINED the staff of the Toronto *Star* in 1904, and through my years on the daily, Charlie Jefferys was one of our best drawing cards—literally and figuratively.

A picture will always outpull a thousand words, but in those days the process of photo-engraving was in its infancy and the now omni-present news photographer was still unheard of. Newspaper illustra-tions for the most part were hand drawn sketches, reproduced in black and white by a line process.

Born in England in 1869, Charles W. Jefferys was apprenticed at the age of eleven to a Toronto lithographing firm where he learned the fundamentals of art and design. After eight years with the art staff of the New York *Herald*, he returned in 1900 to join the *Star*.

Jefferys was a rapid as well as a skilful artist, and was supremely conscious of the meaning of a newspaper deadline. Whether it was a public meeting in Massey Hall with Sir Wilfrid Laurier on the plat-form or an exciting murder mystery, he was always Johnny-on-the-spot. Even if he had to sit up all night to finish it, the *Star* always had an excellent sketch to illustrate its story the next day.

In time, however, he tired of newspaper illustrating and turned himself to picturing Canada's story. His drawings appeared in magazines, histories and school texts, until, with the passing of the years, nearly every outstanding event in our nation's life was portrayed in a Jefferys' sketch.

One of his most famous drawings is that of the martyrdom, in 1649, of Fathers Jean de Brebeuf and Gabriel Lalemant on the banks of Ontario's Sturgeon River. This picture was made to my order to illustrate a story on the Martyrs' Shrine near Midland, which had been written for the *Star Weekly* by Frederick Griffin. The success of that illustration led to an arrangement for a whole series of historical drawings. One appeared every week for several months, a task that would have daunted a less ambitious and tireless worker. It meant endless research before a line was put on paper.

Jeffery's work was done with such devotion to detail that the critics found few faults. He was always storing up material for pictures he hoped to make some day. Everything was filed with the greatest care, and his collection of Canadiana was priceless.

"Some people think I am a terrible crank," he said to me once. "They say I make a fetish of accuracy. Possibly it may look that way, but I really could not work any other way. I just have to know that what I am doing is true, or I cannot do it. And so I spend endless hours in hunting down every last scrap of evidence that I can find. I want to make sure that what I do will not have to be done over again."

How did he compose his pictures and set his characters in such natural relationship? This is what he told me.

"I have long held that there is a natural ground plan for every group of people," said he. "And so the first thing I do is to take a blank sheet of paper and imagine myself looking down on the scene from above. I mark in the four points of the compass. Then if one man is coming from the west I place a dot representing him on the western side of the centre. Another man may be coming from the east to meet him there, and naturally he will be somewhere east of the centre. Then I group the followers of each principal figure around him, each by a dot or 'x' as I think they would naturally stand or sit. Next I draw a circle around them some distance away, and I project myself in imagination on the outside of that circle and slowly walk around it till I come to the position where I think I would get the finest pictorial grouping. And that is how I plan my picture. It is not original with me. There is no great trick about it. The grouping just seems to lay itself out for me before I begin.".

After a lifetime of work on historical subjects Jefferys had another inspiration. He would gather together his studies of Canadian life and history into a series of volumes which The Ryerson Press was eager to publish under the title, *The Picture Gallery of Canadian History*. It was a tremendous task to collect and arrange the 2,000 or more drawings in proper relationship to each other. Some of his best efforts had disappeared, and lay outside Canadian history. Others belonged to publishers for whom he had made them on commission. Everyone was willing to help, however, and a complete set of three volumes was published. No other books of Canadiana contain so much invaluable and irreplaceable material. They cover the national story from 1500 to 1900.

Charlie Jefferys was a gentle and lovable soul. Many artists are jealous of others of their craft who succeed. Not so Jefferys. He was always willing and anxious to encourage beginners and show them the tricks of handling pen or brush.

Though most of his work was done in India ink he was also a master in watercolours and oils. Some magnificent murals on the life of prehistoric man were made by him for the Royal Ontario Museum. Other of his murals are on the walls of the Chateau Laurier and the Manoir Richelieu.

Jefferys was also a writer of graceful and limpid prose. "English is a tool he employed with the same force and facility as distinguished his use of the pencil and the brush," said his biographer William Colgate.

Of all the men who worked with me on the Toronto *Star* the most certain to achieve immortality is Charles W. Jefferys R.C.A., LL.D. who died in 1952. If the way to undying fame is to hitch one's self to something in itself immortal, Charlie Jefferys discovered that secret early when he set himself to reproduce with pen and brush the history of his adopted land. His work will never be equalled, let alone surpassed. It is a tragedy that his genius was bound by human limitations. He should have lived forever as the recorder of Canada's unfolding story.

# 19 ⫷

## *Whimsical Philosopher*

BUT OF ALL THE MEN around the *Star* in the first decade of the twentieth century, the one who had the most influence on me was a short round fellow, fair haired, clean shaven, with a high forehead, twinkling eyes, and a quick friendly smile, who answered to the name of Joe Clark.

If it hadn't been for Joe Clark there might not have been a *Star Weekly,* at least for some years, and it was on that *Weekly* that I was to spend the rest of my time with the *Star.*

No man on the *Star* was ever more loved than Joe. As tolerant as he was good natured, he could get angry but seldom did. His delightful sense of humour made his editorials universally popular. Seldom was there a barb in anything he wrote. With Joe, making friends and influencing people came naturally. The sportsmanship which he showed on the golf course and the cricket green he carried into his daily work. His was a rare and engaging personality.

A product of the country newspaper office, he never lost the freshness which he brought with him from the rolling hills and winding trout streams of rural Ontario. Flesherton, up near Georgian Bay, was Joe's birthplace and it was there he first handled paper and ink. He emerged as a tramp printer, journeying around Ontario from one weekly newspaper office to another, setting type and generally making himself useful.

He loved to tell how he got ready to leave Durham for his first city job.

"Being sixteen at the time, and a man is more important at sixteen than he ever will be again, it seemed that before I got to Toronto I ought to get shaved."

He had never handled a razor before, and soon his face was covered with blood. Suddenly his brother came into the room.

"For a horrible moment he thought I did not want to leave for the city and was trying to commit suicide," said Joe. "He overpowered me, took away the razor, and, with a towel, removed the lather to examine the damage. I arrived in Toronto the next day with strips of sticking plaster all over my face."

About 1887, Joe Clark and his brother Jim bought the Pickering *News,* published in a village not far east of Toronto. That little weekly soon won Province-wide attention for its clever editorials, and W. F. Maclean of the Toronto *Morning World* offered Joe a job. When he arrived in the city he was asked to write some editorials, while another Maclean, a brother of W. F., was on holiday. Joe protested that he wanted to be a reporter not an editor. However, he tried his hand and did so well he was kept at it.

E. E. Sheppard of *Saturday Night,* popular under the name of "Don," soon afterwards added Clark to the staff as his right bower. Joe wrote over the signature "Mac." Together they made a strong team.

It was while he was on *Saturday Night* in 1899 that Clark was first invited to join the *Star.* After a time, when Sheppard died, however, he went back to *Saturday Night* as chief editor, much to J. E. Atkinson's dismay. Later when John Lewis retired as editor-in-chief of the *Star,* Atkinson persuaded Clark to return to his paper. Though Joe never directly told me so, I believe he was often sorry he had exchanged the freedom of his pulpit on *Saturday Night* for the somewhat more restricted atmosphere of the *Star.*

Clark's editorials struck the keynote of the *Star's* policy in its relation to the public. A kindly man himself, he gave people the feeling that the *Star* was a kindly newspaper. His writing often showed a vein of tender sentiment, which was as much a part of his character as his love of fun.

"Joe Clark was J. E. Atkinson's conscience," said one very close to the *Star's* editor. "When Mr. Atkinson was a little worried over the way things were going or things he had done, he would go into Joe's office and talk to him about what he would like to do with the *Star.* And Joe would listen, and perhaps come up with a few ideas which 'J. E. A.' would adopt as his own, and the chief would go away satisfied."

Joe Clark's sense of fun came to the rescue when the strenuous and spectacular fight the *Star* had waged, in the reciprocity election of 1911, ended nonetheless in the defeat of the Laurier government. Everyone was waiting to see what the *Star* would say. Instead of trying to explain the disaster, Clark led off with an editorial on "The Decline of Ping Pong." All Toronto laughed and much of the election bitterness was erased.

The gentleness and courage that underlay his humour are seen in this passage from an editorial, "Marching Men," which he wrote at the time of the death of John R. Bone, the *Star's* veteran managing editor:

Life is for all of us an adventure—a journey from a past that we cannot recall towards a future that we strive to imagine. There are many others with us on the way, all pressing forward, making fair time, getting what pleasure they can from the sunlight, saying little of the anxieties they feel, for the way is long, the urge to keep going must be obeyed. But how or when the journey ends for each one, none can know. As the march proceeds an unseen arrow flies and the comrade by your side goes down. For life is an adventure all along the way.

Joe Clark was a devoted fisherman. The happiest hours of his life were those summer weekends and vacations he spent at his cottage at Go-Home, on the eastern shore of Georgian Bay, where he could enjoy the peace and contentment that an angler finds in communion with nature.

It was there he died, on July 23, 1937.

# 20 ⋘

## The Baby That Wasn't Wanted

THE TORONTO *Star Weekly* was the brain child of J. E. Atkinson. But from the start it met with the indifference or active hostility of most of his associates who were engaged in building up the *Daily Star.* Nevertheless, throughout its early vicissitudes and the years of struggle, when others looked on it as an experiment that could only end in costly failure, Atkinson retained his faith in its future.

He was convinced that a weekend paper, that would compete with the *Sunday World,* would both add to the prestige of the *Daily Star* and provide an additional source of revenue. But uncertainty as to the precise character the new publication should assume added to the precariousness of its infancy.

The idea of Joe Clark, its first editor, was to turn out an unpretentious, friendly journal, something along the lines of the English *T.P.'s Weekly.* Modestly produced on newsprint and without benefit of coloured comics and lavish picture display, it was to be quite different from Toronto's *Sunday World.* It would not aim at a large circulation, and being inexpensively printed, would pay its way from the start. Joe Clark brought Harry W. Jakeway from *Saturday Night* as assistant editor, and placed him in charge of theatre, music, book reviews and other features.

Clark's idea got one week's trial. The first issue was published on April 9, 1910, all on newsprint. There were no comics, and all pictures were printed from standard daily coarse-screen halftones.

Public response was disappointing. Sales seemed to indicate that readers would not pay five cents for a weekend paper both poorly illustrated and lacking a comic section.

Following a conference between J. E. Atkinson and Managing Editor Bone, it was decided to add immediately a four-page picture section, using fine-screen halftones on coated paper. Fred Booth, of Pringle and Booth, news and commercial photographers, was called in to supply local news pictures to supplement the *Star's* outside photographic services. I joined the staff that week, and was placed in charge of the illustrated section.

Sales began to go up, but slowly. The new project had no friends around the *Star* except Atkinson, Bone, Clark, Jakeway and myself, and even Clark was uneasy about the direction in which the paper was headed. He did not like the thought of another paper like the *Sunday World,* with its sensational syndicated feature articles and coloured comic section on the model of New York "yellow journalism" —a term, by the way, deriving from the New York *World's* comic page, which featured the adventures of a character called "The Yellow Kid."

Circulation Manager Bill Argue was expected to sell the *Star Weekly* in competition with the *Sunday World,* and found it a tough assignment. "There's nothing in the *Weekly,*" he complained, "but the street cries of London and Greg Clark's baby." Bob Baker, advertising manager, had to sell space in a paper that had neither the circulation nor the prospects to make it attractive to advertisers. When they did buy space in the *Weekly,* they were apt to compensate by cutting down their lineage in the daily.

By the end of the year circulation had climbed to 16,000. But Joe Clark, who saw his conception of a weekend paper going by the board, asked to be relieved of the editorship. He returned to the daily's editorial page and I was appointed his successor.

My instructions from Atkinson were to produce a weekly paper which would be welcomed in any Canadian home, and which would provide a medium for young Canadian writers in addition to publishing material from those who had already made a name for themselves. At first the budget was small; but eventually, when the *Weekly* got out of the red, I was able to step up our rates to $100 for a story or article —almost as much as *Maclean's Magazine* was then paying. During the depression of the thirties, however, when all expenses had to be cut, our top price dropped to a low of $50.

But the first seven years were full of anxiety. Advertising earnings were insufficient to pay for original and syndicated articles and features, engravings, telegraph tolls, and the one-seventh of *Daily Star* editorial salaries which were charged against the *Weekly*—let alone staff salaries, paper, typesetting and printing, which were supposed to be taken care of by circulation profits, but seldom were.

Eventually the *Weekly* was given its own advertising manager, James T. LaTrobe, who struggled for a while against discouraging odds. He was succeeded by Bob Murray, who did much better, since by that time the paper had added comics and other features, and had attained a circulation that made it more attractive to advertisers.

So much money went down the drain that even Atkinson was worried. But he was still convinced that the *Weekly* could be made to pay, and he refused to listen to suggestions that it be merged with the Saturday edition of the daily.

In 1913, we added comic strips to our *Weekly* features, beginning with The Dream of a Rarebit Fiend, Brick Bodkin's Pa, The Terrors of the Tiny Tads, Uncle Mun, and Mr. Tweedeedle. Three of the five were fairy tales. Our circulation jumped 4,000 to 26,000. Then came the outbreak of the First World War, and we went up by another 11,000. By the war's end, the total was over 67,000.

The tide had turned. Advertising was steadily increasing. The paper was showing a weekly profit of $25 to $450, with only an occasional run of deficits. In the twelve months beginning July, 1919, our circulation jumped from 79,000 to over 122,000. This rapid gain was the result of a general change in editorial policy. Emphasis was being placed on lighter, more entertaining material, especially of a humorous character; short fiction, both original and syndicated, was added; and a press and equipment were installed to produce the picture section by the rotogravure process.

Experience had proved that what the majority of the public wanted in a weekend paper was primarily entertainment. After some years of experiment with a paper which differed widely from the prevailing American type of Sunday paper, it had become clear that if the *Weekly* was to become an asset rather than a liability to its publisher, we must lighten its tone.

The new line of appeal brought the *Weekly* into a stronger competitive position with its rival *Sunday World*. The latter was steadily losing circulation, and its publisher found difficulty in keeping it and his daily *World* in a state of solvency. So confident was Atkinson of the *Weekly's* future that he doubled the selling price from five to ten cents a copy. With the *Sunday World* still selling at the lower figure, circulation of the *Star Weekly* dropped back 20,000 in the first two months to 93,000. But gradually we climbed back. Readers who had deserted us for the cheaper *Sunday World* returned, and, by the end of the year, we had regained all lost ground.

By 1921 the financial position of the *World* and its Sunday edition had become so desperate that its publisher W. F. Maclean decided to sell out to the Douglas brothers, proprietors of the *Mail and Empire*. The latter absorbed the morning *World* in their own paper, and continued to publish the *Sunday World*. I received an invitation from the Douglases to become the editor of the *Sunday World* at a considerable increase in salary. When I mentioned this to Atkinson, he congratulated me, suggested that I would probably have a better future with the *Star Weekly*, but said nothing about salary. I turned down the Douglas' offer, and that week received a bigger pay increase than if I had gone to the *World*.

For good or ill, the importance of the comic strip in attracting readership had assumed proportions that no publisher could ignore. The challenge presented by the *Sunday World* under its new ownership was met by the *Star Weekly* in 1923 with the introduction of eight popular comics, including Bringing Up Father, Barney Google, Clarence, Tillie the Toiler, Polly, Toots and Caspar, Reg'lar Fellers, and Mutt and Jeff. Our extra four pages of comics was too much for the *Sunday World*, which was now running far behind the *Weekly* in sales. Its publishers accepted an offer from Atkinson, and on November 15, 1924, the *Star Weekly* took over the *Sunday World* and its assets.

With its local competition eliminated, circulation of the *Star Weekly* continued to climb. In June of 1928 it reached the 200,000 mark. Still catering to the growing popular demand for comics, the *Weekly* in 1931 enlarged its comic supplement to twelve pages, adding such popular Chicago *Tribune* features as Ella Cinders, The Gumps, Winnie Winkle, Moon Mullins, Gasoline Alley, Little Orphan Annie, and Smitty. Circulation mounted steadily, and in April of 1932, by which time I had been its editor for 21 years, it had risen to 250,000.

From being the weak sister of the *Star* organization, the *Weekly* had become the chief provider. When the *Weekly* was launched in 1910, the daily's sales were 69,953. By the spring of 1920, the *Star Weekly* had caught up to and passed the daily for keeps. From then on it forged steadily ahead. Atkinson's faith in the dark days had been justified to the full.

# 21 «««

## Riding a Spirited Steed

Not until the end of the First World War, when the circulation had reached 67,000, was there any expansion in the *Star Weekly's* editorial staff. Till then it consisted only of Harry W. Jakeway and myself. No editor ever had a more faithful or harder working assistant. With excellent judgment he sifted the tares from the wheat in incoming manuscripts, and occasionally wrote feature articles, besides looking after theatre, music, and other regular features.

At last the day came when I was empowered to add to the salaried staff. Beginning with Gregory Clark, I gathered about me a group of gifted writers and artists whose high level of excellence I dare to suggest has seldom, if ever, been equalled in the history of Canadian journalism. These included Jimmy Frise the cartoonist, Frederick Griffin, Charles Vining, Robert C. Reade, and John Herries McCulloch. Among our more or less regular contributors were in addition Ernest Hemingway, R. E. Knowles, Chief Buffalo Child Long Lance, Gordon Sinclair, Morley Callaghan, Merrill Denison, Arthur D. Kean, Mary Lowrey, Claire Wallace, Nina Moore Jamieson, Nellie McClung. In the course of time, many of them were to be borrowed or taken over by the daily to function as the most spectacular group of world travellers and feature writers Canada had ever produced.

Every Wednesday, after the paper was off the press, we had a staff luncheon, at which outside contributors were guests. We discussed the current issue, analyzed its merits and defects, and laid plans for new projects. At one of these luncheons the guest of honour was Vilhjalmur Stefansson, the explorer, who provided frozen reindeer steaks for the meat course, and afterwards caused some uneasiness by informing us that they had been cut from a carcass killed three years before. One day Atkinson was our guest, and was so impressed with the way his staff spent their lunch hours that a generous increase in salaries followed.

Pungent paragraphs for the editorial page were written by R. C. Reade, a man of brilliant gifts whom I had met when we were fellow students at Woodstock College. He was one of the first Canadian Rhodes scholars from the University of Toronto, and, on his return from Oxford, joined the staff of the *Daily Star*. Transferred from the *Daily* to the *Weekly*, he became a regular contributor of feature articles.

For the first few years, the only regular outside contributor to the *Weekly* was Arthur R. Jones, a stout, ruddy-faced Englishman who was extraordinarily well informed on British political and social affairs. He was a Tory by conviction, but had so far mastered the art of objective writing that he could present a convincing case for socialism.

A feature which became very popular was the department devoted to motoring and motorists. This was conducted for some years by Warren B. Hastings, later editor of *The Canadian Motorist* and now general manager of the Ontario Motor League. Subsequently the department was in charge of W. Frank Prendergast, now assistant to the president of The Imperial Oil Company.

One *Star Weekly* feature was literally so successful that it had to be discontinued without notice. It was conducted by F. D. Jacobs, an Ottawa civil servant who was an expert graphologist. Character analysis from handwriting specimens sent in by readers was offered without charge, and in less than a month the letters were rolling in faster than they could be answered. The original column and a half allotment was extended to three columns, then to four, and before long the department was occupying a full page. With letters arriving in sackfuls, and answers two months behind, we decided to discontinue the feature. Over 5,000 letters went unanswered.

During the First War, we offered prizes for anecdotes by returned soldiers. These little tales, humorous and tragic, were illustrated by staff artists, and created almost as much interest as Mr. Jacob's graphology.

Perhaps our most popular regular feature was the Page About People, made up of short character sketches and stories about well known Canadians. Two dollars was paid for each item used with longer stories bought on space rates. Most had a humorous angle.

A syndicated series of essays by British writers, entitled "My Religion," was followed up by a request to prominent Canadians for similar statements, but the response was disappointing. Few were willing to discuss their beliefs in public.

Sir Henry Thornton, then president of the C.N.R., begged off with the confession that "I have quite enough trouble running the national railway without stepping into the religious arena . . . a subject full of high explosives for me." Henri Bourassa dodged adroitly with "to do justice to the subject, especially in the English language, would require an amount of time and serene reflection which I have not at my disposal." Principal Arthur Currie of McGill University, commander of the Canadian Army in World War I, admitted frankly, "the idea does not appeal to me." John Bracken, then Prime Minister of Manitoba, and later leader of the Progressive-Conservative Party, replied: "I wish to compliment you on the idea . . . but regret that pressure of other work will prevent me taking on an engagement of this kind."

But two well known Canadian women did accede to my request—Magistrate Emily F. Murphy of Edmonton, better known by her pen name of "Janey Canuck," and the novelist, Mrs. Nellie McClung. I preserved these sentences from Mrs. Murphy's article:

I have come to know God as never before because I have ceased defining him. My creed has become a simple one and may be summarized: Love is the fulfilling of the law; 'love, ever active, never still,' is the irresistible and compelling force of the universe. As a religious certainty I have come to know that all is good, that whatever is, is best.

And this from the contribution of Mrs. McClung:

Religion is a bridge and as such must have two qualifications. It must carry much weight and it must endure in the tide of great waters. If it has these two qualifications then it is a good bridge irrespective of size, colour or shape. It is a deadly sin, I believe, to lay an axe to another man's bridge. I love the Bible for its stately music and the elegance of its diction, and the words of Christ have the power to set all the bells in my heart ringing.

For some years we printed the delightful children's stories of Thornton W. Burgess, who also took over the editorship of Old Mother Nature's Club, a department inaugurated by C. M. Caniff, a gentle and kindly man who wrote delightfully about the birds and animals of Ontario.

Serial rights were secured on outstanding books. Among these were Lytton Strachey's *Queen Victoria,* Maurice Hindus' *Humanity Uprooted,* Remarque's *All Quiet on the Western Front,* and Stefansson's *The Friendly Arctic.* We also ran Margot Asquith's autobiographical articles which were causing a sensation in British political and social circles. The syndicates supplied us with articles by T. P. O'Connor, stories by Ring Lardner, and, during the First World War, the brilliant war commentaries of Frank H. Simonds. A fine series of articles on his war experiences by Canon F. G. Scott was shared with a Montreal paper.

Five artists were kept busy on the *Weekly* during the later years of my editorship. Jimmy Frise had made his Birdseye Centre one of the most popular features of the paper. Galbraith O'Leary, a charming Irish lad with a delightful sense of humour, did illustrations in pen and wash. "Deacon" Bill Johnston worked on layouts for the rotogravure section. Victor Child did story illustrations and layouts. Among the free lance artists we employed were many already in the top rank, and others have since won fame. These included Franz Johnston, Manley Macdonald, Arthur Lismer, C. W. Jefferys, E. J. Dinsmore, Fred H. Varley, J. E. H. MacDonald, Franklin Arbuckle, Tom Mitchell, L. A. C. Panton, H. W. McCrea, Estelle M. Kerr, Fergus Kyle, Grant H. MacDonald, Lydia Fraser and Charles Comfort.

It was a great privilege to have more or less regular contacts with writers and artists of such varied gifts, and to be in a position to provide them with a medium for the exercise of their talents. I am glad to think that the money they earned in the service of the *Star Weekly* was, for many of them, an important factor in the period when they were laying the foundations of success and fame.

Bill Law, a hard-working, conscientious Scot, and an excellent draughtsman, served from time to time on the *Weekly's* staff of artists. While working as a free-lance, he completed a series of action paintings of Canadian game fish for the Dominion Government Travel Bureau which was one of the finest things of its kind ever done in Canada.

Franz Johnston I got to know better in later days, after I had moved to Midland. In nearby Wyebridge he had remodelled an old community hall into a fascinating dwelling containing rare pieces of European furniture. Most of the work he did for the *Star Weekly* consisted of small ink sketches and decorative tailpieces. He had great versatility as a painter, and later became one of Canada's most popular and best paid artists.

When the *Star's* new skyscraper building was just about completed, Johnston suggested to Atkinson that he submit a plan of decoration. He worked for a full week on such a plan, and then took it to the *Star's* chief. It was a complete scheme of ornamentation, whose execution would have cost thousands of dollars.

Atkinson, much pleased, reached for his cheque book and began to write a cheque for $50. Johnston was aghast. "But the plan is worth much more than that," he exclaimed. He had decided to ask a fee of at least $200.

"That is what I think it is worth," said Atkinson.

"Very well," replied Johnston, picking up the sketch.

"No, you don't," countered the publisher. "That sketch belongs to me. It is a picture of my building which I commissioned you to draw."

"It may be your building," retorted Johnston, "but it is my sketch." He picked up the drawing and walked out without waiting for the *Star's* publisher to raise his bid. He did no more work for the paper for some years.

At one time I had a large painting of Johnston's hanging over the desk in my *Star Weekly* office. It showed a forest ranger rounding a curve of a northern river in a canoe whose sail was a red Hudson's Bay blanket. Bordering the river banks was a tall stand of pine to which the summer haze gave a purple hue.

One day Mr. Atkinson, noticing the picture, remarked: "I have never seen purple trees." I reported this comment to Johnston. "Ah," said the artist, "doesn't he wish he could!"

After I left the *Weekly* in 1933, the paper went in heavily for wild animals. Its new boss, Harry Hindmarsh, was fond of stories about lions, tigers, bears, and other ferocious creatures. Issue after issue saw snarling leopards leaping from trees on their prey, angry elephants charging through the jungle, howling wolves chasing frantic deer, eagles swooping down on helpless children, or boa constrictors squeezing their victims to death.

One day I met artist Gal O'Leary. With a serious face he told me the *Star Weekly* was about to suspend publication.

"How's that?" I asked, sensing some fun.

"Our gorilla has got away," he replied, "and Hindmarsh doesn't know what to do next."

The transformation, which had taken place over the years, in the editorial and pictorial content of the *Star Weekly* did not have the unanimous endorsement of the Atkinson family. Mrs. J. E. Atkinson differed materially in her outlook from many of her husband's circulation-minded executives.

While still a reporter on the *Globe,* Atkinson had married Elmina Elliott, whose daily column over the pen-name of Madge Merton was a popular feature of the paper. Born on her grandfather's farm near Oakville, Ontario, she had worked on *Saturday Night,* and had come to the *Globe* a year after young Atkinson joined its staff. After their marriage in 1891, she continued to write her column, and when her husband became managing editor of the Montreal *Herald,* she edited its woman's page. For some years after Atkinson assumed direction of the *Star,* she contributed to it a regular Saturday feature over the old pen-name.

Mrs. Atkinson was a serious-minded woman, and her writings dealt with nature, books, and social and charitable movements rather than with problems of the lovelorn and the gossip of "society," as did those of so many contemporary women columnists. She did much to promote interest in woman's suffrage, and was keenly interested in such benevolent projects as the Star Fresh Air and Santa Claus Funds, or anything that would better the condition of the poor.

She had no ambition to mingle in fashionable society, and little interest in fine clothes, though she dressed becomingly and in good taste. She was not given to small talk, and her genuine kindliness was masked by a certain austerity of manner. In her simply-furnished home she entertained few guests, and devoted her time to her work and to her husband and two children. She believed thoroughly in the power of kindness, and when her husband asked her advice on any course of action which affected other people, she would say, "What is the kind thing to do?"

Her idealism undoubtedly helped to influence her husband's policies, and in the early days she had a profound affect on the character of the *Star.* However, her sympathies were not as wide as his, nor did she always appreciate the need to appeal to popular tastes in order to build circulation.

The *Star Weekly* struggled along gamely for over three years without the aid of comic strips, largely, I believe, because of Mrs. Atkinson's dislike of them. Shortly after we had introduced our first comic features, artistically drawn and mostly of a fairy tale quality, my wife and I called at the Atkinson home. The talk turned to the comics and Mrs. Atkinson expressed her disapproval quite vigorously. I came to their defense, and it was soon necessary for Atkinson to come to mine.

"My dear," he said, "I am not running a Sunday School paper."

"I rather wish you were," she replied.

The subject was quickly dropped. But as the years went by the fairy tale comics were displaced by more vigorous flesh and blood features.

I have sometimes wondered whether Mrs. Atkinson was respon- sible for naming the *Star Weekly,* though it is true that neither of them liked the idea of a "Sunday" paper. The Chief always refused to listen to suggestions from the business office that the name be changed to *Sunday Star.*

She did, however, change one name—her husband's. It was not until after his marriage to Elmina Elliott that Joseph Atkinson acquired a middle initial. It happened this way.

Those were days when calling cards were much in vogue. Mrs. Atkinson thought they should have some, and democratic Joseph agreed. But plain "Joseph Atkinson" did not look quite right, and certainly "J. Atkinson" was too stiff. To give the name balance a middle initial was needed. What would go well with Joseph? Why not "E."—Elmina's initial?

And so "Joseph E. Atkinson" made its appearance. The three initials "J. E. A." were to become as familiar around the newspaper world as they were around the *Star.*

Most readers will have forgotten that before Mrs. Atkinson's death pictures of scantily garbed women were taboo in the *Star.* Once, before the days of rotogravure, I printed on the front page of the picture section the photograph of a girl lying on the sand beach of Centre Island. By today's standards she was conservatively clad, wearing a one-piece bathing suit with short skirt. But on Monday morning I was called to Atkinson's office. He said the picture was most objectionable, and he did not want to see anything like it in the *Weekly* again. Since he must have seen the picture before the presses began to roll, I feel sure it was Mrs. Atkinson who was really responsible for the reprimand. In later years, of course, such pictures became a commonplace in both the *Star* and the *Star Weekly.*

After a long battle against illness, which lasted for over a year, death came to Mrs. Atkinson in 1931. Throughout she maintained her customary cheerfulness and courage. It must have brought her great happiness to see her husband occupying top place in the Canadian newspaper world, and the *Star* installed in its skyscraper home. She had been a sustaining influence in his business, as well as a devoted helpmate in the home.

Back in 1908, as Madge Merton, she had written in one of her newspaper columns:

> Your better self you call your good angel. For days and days you do not hear from her. Sometimes you think she is dead, or you are, and then something warms your heart and sings softly and argues with you, or shames and advises you. And she, one of the best of the good fairies, has come back to you again. There are people who have lost their good angels, and the way is very dreary for them afterwards.

Without a doubt J. E. Atkinson lost his "good angel" when his wife died, and the way was dreary for him afterwards. He withdrew into himself, and became a lonely man in his newspaper household.

# 22 ««

## Five Foot Two, Eyes of Blue

ALTHOUGH THE *Star Weekly* lost its first Clark when Joseph T. returned
to his post as editor-in-chief of the *Daily*, it gained an equally famous
member of the family when his eldest son Gregory became our first,
full-time staff writer.

Greg was a cub reporter on the *Daily Star* before World War I.
He had spent two years in the freshman class at the University of
Toronto before trading higher education for journalism. Mathematics
completely baffled him. To Greg Clark it was just a lot of lies.

"They told me A equalled B, and that X plus Y equalled Z. But
I knew it wasn't so. It couldn't be," he declared. "A doesn't equal B
and it never has."

One day he brought into my office a story he had written, a bit
of fancy with a streak of whimsical humour. I liked it but had to tell
him that, as he was a member of the *Daily* staff, I could not pay him
anything extra for his work. That didn't bother Greg. He said he
would be glad to have it used and would bring me more. And despite
the kidding of his fellow scribes that he was working for nothing, he
did. He learned to write by writing.

Soon Greg's little yarns were a regular *Weekly* feature. Jimmy
Frise, then a retouch artist on the *Daily*, illustrated them with small
cartoons, beginning a long and nationally known partnership.

World War I, however, intervened. Enlisting as a private, Greg
fought valiantly, won a commission, was awarded the Military Cross
at Vimy Ridge and came home a major. He also came home convinced
that there was more money in advertising than there was in reporting.
However when I suggested that he join the *Weekly* as a staff writer,

and managing editor John Bone concurred, he agreed to return to the *Star*.

Greg had ideas galore, and I leaned on him heavily for advice. The *Star Weekly* took on a new flavour. Entertainment and humour were featured. "Boss," he used to say to me, "come up to the corner of Queen and Yonge Streets and have a look at the people who buy our paper. Then you will know what to put into it." The original idea of a small journal of literature and opinion—Greg's father's dream —had long since been dropped. Our circulation sights were set high and the younger Clark was now helping develop the very type of newspaper which his father had earlier opposed.

Whimsical weekly sketches about his young children were among Greg's most popular contributions to the *Weekly*. I counted a week lost without one. His stunt stories soon had our readers rollicking. We would work out some ridiculous idea and then literally try it out on the public. One day Greg and the dignified Main Johnson, later editor of the *Weekly*, were walking together past the King Edward Hotel, then Toronto's chief hostelry. Greg took off his hat and let it fall to the pavement. Dropping to his knees, he crouched down beside it. Gingerly he lifted one corner of the hat, then slammed it down hard. A group of passers-by stopped. Main Johnson, mightily embarrassed, flushed, and walked hurriedly on. Once more Greg peeped excitedly under his hat as if it contained something alive. Again he slammed it to the pavement. Soon a hundred curious people were crowded around and the throng was increasing rapidly. Finally, just as the police were about to disperse the mob, Greg nonchalantly picked up his hat, placed it on his head at the usual rakish angle, and strolled off. It made an amusing story.

We ran this type of yarn about once a month. Sometimes Charlie Vining, later president of the Canadian Newsprint Association, or Merrill Denison, who has become an internationally known author and playwright, were brought in as partners for Greg in these farcical adventures. Occasionally they took turns at doing the writing. Here is an extract I remember from a sketch by Vining, entitled "Everybody Happy," in which he attempted to interview Greg Clark in the accredited newspaper style:

"Do you mind telling me, Greg," started Vining, "how you ever got to be a major in the army?"

"By not getting killed," was the quick retort. "They could not help making me a major because there was nobody else left."

"What did you do in the war?" Vining countered.

"I was the champion athlete of the whole brigade," said Clark. "I could jump higher, dig quicker, and lie flatter than anyone in the brigade—including our colonel."

Vining then told Greg that he would have to give an accurate description of him.

"What would you say?" asked Clark.

Vining's reply was as long as Greg was short. "I would just tell what you look like. Five feet, two inches tall, tousled iron grey hair, large head, small face, green shirt, red tie, big clothes, shoes not shining, pockets always bulging with old letters which are never answered, hat over one ear, small glittering blue eyes behind a screen of long straight lashes, humorous terrier brows, acquisitive nose, hard mouth if you take off that straggly moustache, loud voice, big stride, cold hand, fine telephone manner, ready promise but—"

"That's a libel!" protested Greg. "You'd get the paper into trouble. That's my character not my appearance."

But Vining went on unperturbed. "There would be something about your habit of procrastination, your fixed rule never to be any place on time no matter how important it is, the way you mismanage your money, and your artfulness in bluffing about things you don't know anything about."

Greg, at least in the story, subsided.

In later years Greg Clark and Jimmy Frise collaborated in these stunt stories but as time went on they originated largely in Clark's head, and were filled with his original and entertaining philosophy. Frise did the cartoon illustrations and many of the sketches he made looked more like Greg than Greg does himself.

Clark is a grand writer but I have often wished that he could write as vividly as he can talk. He is one of the most entertaining conversationalists I have ever known. One has to hear a yarn from Greg's lips to get the full value of his descriptive gifts and his ability to mimic. He gestures with his whole body, and his whole body laughs.

But not all Greg's life has been on the funny side. In World War II he was sent overseas as a war correspondent for the *Daily Star*. He was in France just after "D" Day with the Canadian army when his son, Lieutenant Murray Clark, the pride and joy of his father's heart, was killed in action. Greg stood by the grave as his lad was buried. His mind may well have returned that day to another like it in the First World War when, after the Canadians had captured Vimy Ridge, Greg was called on to conduct the funeral service of the men of his company who had fallen. Assembling the survivors around the mass grave, Captain Clark commenced the service from memory. When he came to the place for the prayer, his mind went blank. He could not recall a word. Suddenly—he knew not how—the prayer he had learned at his mother's knee came back, and he began:

> "Now I lay me down to sleep,
> I pray the Lord my soul to keep,
> If I should die before I wake,
> I pray the Lord my soul to take."

It was a curious prayer for a military burial but the men who had seen their comrades die were not critical. Perhaps that prayer carried them home. Certainly it reached Heaven.

Naturally when Murray was killed, Greg wanted to get home at once to be with his wife. A cabled request to Hindmarsh at the *Star* brought no reply. Mrs. Clark suffered a nervous breakdown. Greg's brother Joe, himself a veteran of World War I, and in charge of public relations for the Canadian armed services at Ottawa, tried twice without success to reach President Atkinson. Then through military headquarters he secured an order for Greg's immediate return.

When, two years later, Greg learned of his brother's inability to secure the *Star's* co-operation, he immediately submitted his resignation and, while continuing for a time to do his regular "Greg and Jim" story for the *Weekly,* turned his main energies to radio. He had lost his love for the newspaper and, as he told me, "was tired of being a work horse."

"Now I know where I am going to be tomorrow night," he continued. "I can plan my week with reasonable certainty. I can live with my wife and family, and know when I say goodbye in the morning that I shall be home at night. When I was a reporter I never knew five minutes ahead what I was going to be doing in the next five minutes. A murder, a train wreck, a plane crash, or any one of a hundred things might happen. The bell would ring, and the old firehorse would have to rush out and get the story, write it, shoot it into the office, and then get back into the stall waiting for the next alarm.

"That sort of thing had to stop. I enjoyed it while I was young but there came a day when I dreaded assignments given me, particularly those which sent me far from home for weeks and months at a time."

When in the autumn of 1946 Greg was asked by the Montreal *Standard*, rival of the *Star Weekly*, whether he would transfer his weekly feature to that paper, he talked the matter over with Jimmy Frise. They decided to make the jump together.

"In accordance with established *Star* custom of firing men on Christmas Eve," said Greg, telling me about it afterwards, "we delayed sending in our resignations so that they would not be received until the day before Christmas." Overtures from the *Star* were refused, and Clark and Frise began work with the *Standard* in January, 1947.

The fundamental factor in the prompt acceptance of the *Standard* offer was simply that Greg and Jim were delighted that an up-and-coming publication, manned by young men and under a young publisher, had seen fit to make them an offer at all. It flattered their egos. They felt they had no future security with the *Star Weekly*.

Frise's death only a year and a half later was a terrific blow to Greg. He and Jim had been bosom pals. Without the aid of his friend Greg had little heart to carry on. He continued writing the humorous feature for a year or more, but finally turned to other work. He is now associate editor of *Week-end*, a colorgravure and comic magazine, which is sold with the Saturday editions of leading daily papers across Canada, and has a million circulation. He also writes a syndicated column for a number of Canadian dailies.

On the study wall of his home hangs a receipted bill from the *Star* for the death notice of his father J. T. Clark, editor-in-chief of the *Daily*. The bill arrived at his home the day of the funeral. Hopping mad, yet seeing its possibilities, Greg jumped in his car, drove down to the office, paid the bill, had it receipted and framed. He has had no end of fun showing that receipt to his friends.

"Of course," he always tells them, "I know it was an error. It went out as a matter of office routine. But I am glad I paid it just the same." Business manager Fred Tait pleaded with Greg to return the receipt but was refused.

This ability to turn anything to fun is one of the many likeable characteristics of this Peter Pan of Canadian journalism. He just won't grow up or grow old.

Clark could have followed in his father's footsteps had he wished. He was earlier invited by Atkinson to become an editorial writer, but the prospect did not appeal to him. It seemed a stuffy occupation for one who enjoyed freedom to move about as much as did Greg.

But if he refused his father's editorial mantle he did inherit his love for angling and for the clear waters, rocky islands, and winding inlets of the eastern Georgian Bay. At his cottage on Go-Home Bay, Greg is truly at home. All the local fish he knows by their first names. And I somehow suspect the familiarity is mutual.

# 23 ⬅⬅⬅

## "Birdseye Center" Was Real

PICTURE A FRANK, open-faced village boy who was never spoiled by life in the big city, and you have Jimmy Frise (*Fry-z*), creator of "Birdseye Center." After thirty-eight years in Toronto Jimmy belonged as much to his native Port Perry as he did the day he left the shores of Lake Scugog.

No member of the *Star Weekly* staff was more loved by its hundreds of thousands of readers than was Jim. His was the paper's most popular comic feature. "Birdseye Center" was merely another name for Port Perry, but it fitted hundreds of provincial hamlets.

Jim deserved that affection. He was personally a most lovable man. Simple, genuine, unaffected, unassuming, he was incapable of doing a mean thing. He could get angry if really pushed, but, for the most part, life for him was serene and happy.

Frise was uninhibited in his selection of friends and acquaintances. Greg Clark wrote that "he was totally incapable of discrimination amongst humanity. He made no distinction between the useful and the useless, the good and the bad, the worthy and unworthy. Standing around his drawing easel might be big shots of the advertising agencies, race track touts, country editors, pool sharks, elders or deacons, or nameless bums in quest of the unfailing handout. If you had two legs and stood even partly upright you were a man, and Jim gave you his whole gentle, courteous and warm attention." He would work hours of overtime rather than dismiss some one who came to gossip or kibitz.

When Jim came to Toronto he had no definite ambition. As a matter of fact he never did have. He merely wanted a job where he could draw funny pictures. He sent some samples of his work to John

R. Bone at the *Star*. *Bone* had no need for a humorous artist, but he did want a photo retoucher. Jim took the proferred job, though painting out unessential details of portraits, and strengthening eyes, eyebrows, lips, and hair, as well as drawing "X marks the spot" diagrams, was no more exciting then than it is today.

Frise did the retouching faithfully but, whenever he had a spare moment, he drew amusing little figures in black and white. It was at this time that Gregory Clark began to write for the *Weekly* his tales of the curious characters he met on the city streets. I asked Jim to illustrate them. His clever drawings provided just the needed touch.

In the First World War, Frise, like Clark, joined up as a private. Serving with the artillery, Jim had one of the fingers on his left hand blown off by exploding shrapnel. He was invalided home and came back to the *Star*.

I discovered that his salary was being charged to the *Weekly* and my request that his time be given wholly to that paper was granted. We were then carrying a syndicated half-page comic feature in black and white drawn by W. E. Hill and entitled "Among Us Mortals." It was a Chicago Tribune product, and consisted of a series of drawings depicting humorous character studies of all sorts of folks. Though more American than Canadian in atmosphere, it went over well.

The idea struck me that Jimmy Frise, if given a chance, could produce just as good a cartoon but one which would be distinctively Canadian. When I spoke to him about it, with characteristic modesty he declared it impossible. He said he never could keep it up week after week. But after some urging he agreed to try. His first series of drawings was largely a Canadian adaptation of "Among Us Mortals." Reader reaction was overwhelmingly favourable but still Frise wasn't convinced. That long stretch of 52 weeks which makes a year looked frightening. Moreover Jim never believed that his work was really good. He would have gladly given it up at any time. He thought we were just being kind to his "Life's Little Comedies" as the feature was first called.

Gradually the original plan which called for a number of drawings, based on a series of more or less unrelated incidents, was dropped in favour of one large sketch with a single theme. The latter's locale was often a mythical village called "Birdseye Center," and the feature soon adopted that name.

Lest anyone think I claim too much credit for initiating Frise's famous cartoon, let me say that once started, the responsibility for the achievement belonged wholly to him. His were the ideas and his the drawings.

Deadlines were the bane of Jimmy Frise's life. Often he would sit and stare for hours at his drawing board. But the ideas would not come. Or he would make a start and, after some hours of work, tear up what he had done. He was his own keenest critic and not easily satisfied.

Sometimes at the close of office hours on the day before press day, his weekly cartoon was still not begun. He would sit up until nearly dawn, snatch an hour of sleep, and bring it down half finished in the morning. Press deadline was 2 p.m. At twelve noon the nervous foreman of the engraving department would be at Jim's shoulders to ward off all intruders. There was many a time the completed engraving reached the stereotyping department and the presses at 1.59 p.m. On such occasions Jimmy worried himself sick and kept the rest of us frantic. But, despite all the last minute rush, I must confess that the engravings of an American cartoon which I always kept ready as a possible substitute had to be used only once.

Neither Atkinson nor Bone could understand why Jimmy's drawings could not be ready earlier. And they did not hesitate to say so—in repeated memoranda. But Frise was constitutionally opposed to schedules, and he stayed that way through my years on the *Weekly*.

Recognizing the possibility that Jimmy might sometime decide to seek new and greener pastures, the *Star* protected itself by copyrighting "Birdseye Center." When the time did come for Jim to jump to the Montreal *Standard* he was denied the privilege of using the "Birdseye Center" title, but the *Star* could not prevent his taking with him the characters he had made famous. Old Archie and the Moose, Pigskin Peters, Eli Doolittle and others were all transferred to "Juniper Junction," by which name the Frise cartoon was known in the *Standard*.

Jimmy was a genius with his pen. He could handle serious subjects as well as humour in black and white. He had a fine gift of proportion and was a master of light and shade. But it was as a humourist he was supreme. Some humour is unkind. Jimmy's never was. And his followers will never forget the little dogs which dashed about madly in many a cartoon.

It is a great pity that no collection of his cartoons was put into book form. He was oblivious to the possible long-term earning power of his drawings and handed out originals freely to his friends. Frise could have made a fortune had he moved to the United States. His unique gifts would have brought him contracts from big syndicates. Jim, however, was a happy Canadian, and he wanted his children to grow up that way.

This country boy had one great weakness. He loved to play the horses. He just could not resist putting money on a "sure thing." When spring and the races came around, Jim would slip away early in the afternoon to the track, and by night, as often as not, was completely broke. No matter how often and how much he lost, hope sprang eternal in his breast. The sound of the galloping dominoes was also music to his ears and the dice cost him plenty.

Jimmy Frise's death from a heart attack on June 13, 1948, while he was still in his prime, was a national loss. Canada needed him badly at a time when our people spend so many hours studying the allegedly humourous antics of a lot of American characters who do not really belong to our civilization. "Birdseye Center" and its successor, "Juniper Junction," were genuine Canadiana.

When Gregory Clark phoned to tell me of Jim's death, he said, "A great gentleman has passed on." He was right. James Llewellyn Frise was also a great Canadian. No university ever honoured itself by conferring on him an honorary degree, though any Canadian institution of learning might well have done so. A man who can make a whole nation laugh with wholesome fun is worthy of any college's highest distinction. If there had been a "Doctor of Humour" available, Jimmy would have easily earned it.

# 24 ⋘

## *Five Star Reporter*

FRED GRIFFIN was the second man to be added as a writer to the permanent staff of the *Star Weekly*. He joined the *Star* as assistant to the librarian, Jerry Elder. Soon he began submitting stories to the *Weekly*, which I liked and used. Later he spent two years as a reporter on the *Daily*. I coveted him for the *Weekly* and finally got him on my staff.

He could always be depended upon to turn in a good story, well written and packed with information. Though lacking in humour, he had a warm heart that sympathized with human suffering, and a gift for pathos. His wide and rich vocabulary and fine feeling for words made him a master of the telling phrase. And he was never satisfied till he got to the bottom of a story.

The trouble was that the *Daily* was constantly drafting his services. Often he would be off on these assignments for a week or ten days.

In 1933 he visited Russia and afterwards made a book out of his experiences entitled *Soviet Scene*. During the thirties he covered many of the important events in Canada and the United States. His second book, *Variety Show*, told of the famous people he had interviewed, among them Churchill, Roosevelt, de Valera, Kerensky, Stalin and Lindbergh.

Griffin prided himself on being the type of reporter who reports facts without taking sides. He never sought to be an interpreter nor a propagandist for any viewpoint. He always played fair with his sources of information. The people he talked to knew he would deal honestly with them, and never betray a confidence.

Being Irish, he was temperamental. When he did a good job he coveted appreciation. If it came, he beamed. If it did not, he was depressed. Sometimes when he brought in a particularly fine piece of work and I did not go through it immediately, he would flare up and go away in a black mood.

The only time I knew him to flunk an assignment was when editor Main Johnson sent him to Cornwall to get a story on fairies. Main was sure the Irish folk in that region must believe in the "little people." Fred seemed a natural choice for the job, but Main had difficulty in selling him the idea. Finally Fred agreed to try. He took the train to Cornwall, got off at the station, and boarded the next train back. "I just couldn't make a damn fool of myself," he explained.

At the time of his death he had been home only a short while after five years as a war correspondent with the *Daily Star,* with only two or three intermissions. The experience took a severe toll of his nerves and physical strength. He stuck it out, but at last cabled home asking to be relieved. Back came the suggestion that he make a world tour, taking as much time and writing whatever and whenever he pleased, and with no restrictions on expense. He refused the offer. He was exhausted and homesick.

There is a story to the effect that, on his return, Griffin went to pay his respects to President J. E. Atkinson, and that, after a pleasant chat, the latter asked: "Well, Frederick, did you enjoy yourself?"

"I certainly did, Mr. Atkinson," Fred replied.

"Then why," asked the old man, "did you come home so soon?"

Fred gasped, and left the room utterly deflated. He had given everything he had, and this was the thanks he got.

It was shortly after this I saw him for the last time. We chatted in his familiar corner. The war had left its mark. His face was flushed and lined, and he looked tired and dispirited. He was doing unimportant work, and he hated it. Griffin was made for the big story.

Five days later in January, 1946, he died of a heart attack. He was only fifty-six.

# 25 ⫷⫷⫷

## Errors of My Way

SELDOM DOES IT PAY an editor to blow his own horn. But when he does, he often gets a lot of attention.

I remember when, simply by blowing a horn on Toronto's King Street at midday on November 7, 1918, I sent a whole city into an uproar.

The First World War was ending. Negotiations for a German surrender were in progress in a railway car in France's Forest of Compiegne. News of the cessation of hostilities was expected any minute and in the *Star* the telegraph editor scanned each despatch with feverish excitement.

It was one o'clock and, on my way to lunch, I dropped by the wire room. Over the telegraph came this message: FLASH. ARMISTICE SIGNED. WAR OVER.

I ran back to my office, grabbed a horn which I had stored away in my desk against this hour, and ran bareheaded down the main street of Toronto, blowing it as loudly as I could. People stared at me as if I were mad. And I was. I shouted: "Armistice signed! War's over!" Other people started to shout and cheer. In ten minutes all down town Toronto was on the streets, dancing and yelling.

But, after a brief two hours of celebration, came a second wire stating that the first announcement had been premature. The war was still on. Quickly the excitement died, and at least one newspaper editor felt very foolish.

But I wasn't the only one. Owen McGillicuddy of the *Globe and Mail* tells how the false report upset the Supreme Court of Ontario. He was reporting court that day for the *Star*. The afternoon session had just begun when he received word of the supposed armistice. McGillicuddy scribbled a brief note and handed it to Chief Justice R. M. Meredith, noted for his rather pompous decorum. To his amazement, Meredith halted the trial then in progress, rose to his feet and solemnly announced:

I have just received word of the greatest importance. An armistice has been signed and the war is over. This court can sit no longer today. I declare it adjourned.

Whereupon McGillicuddy, released from his day's duties, got a bright idea. John Philip Sousa and his band were in Toronto to give a concert in Massey Hall. Why not invite Sousa to march along King Street to the *Star* office, playing a victory march. McGillicuddy immediately got in touch with Sousa's publicity man and, in the wild enthusiasm which had pervaded the city, Sousa consented. In a few minutes the white uniformed bandsmen, led by the famous conductor, were swinging along to the *Star*, playing with might and main. A huge crowd closed about them, calling for encore after encore. Sousa kept playing until the news broke that the armistice report was false.

But the *Star*'s management was tickled pink. "The finest bit of public relations work around here in years," commented Hindmarsh, McGillicuddy's boss. "Would you like to take two weeks' holidays?" "Sure," the latter replied. "I'd like to take my wife to New York. How about expenses?" "We'll look after that," Hindmarsh said. "Go home and get ready."

Erroneous reports, however, do not always have such a happy ending, especially when they result in libel suits.

If there is anything an editor dreads, it is a libel suit. And even the most innocent, kindly-minded editor may wake up some morning and find a writ on his doorstep. Though he may be absolutely within his rights, such suits are nuisances and, even when successfully defended, cost his paper a heap of money.

Three times I have figured in libel actions, and two of them occurred during my editorship of the *Star Weekly*.

The first resulted from a carelessly-written heading which left the newspaper no defence. In February, 1915, Charles Albert Massey was shot dead on the doorstep of his Toronto home. A domestic servant, Carrie Davis, claimed she killed her employer in self defence and won an acquittal from the jury.

She was but one of a number of women who had been recently freed on murder charges and I asked a reporter to write a story about them. His story was all right but the heading I put on it all wrong. I first wrote ONTARIO IS EASY ON WOMEN CHARGED WITH MURDER. But the line was too long and, in an unwary moment, I shortened it to ONTARIO IS EASY ON MURDERESSES. Miss Davis promptly sued the *Star* for libel. There was, of course, no defence. She was not a murderess. She had been found not guilty. There was nothing to do but negotiate a settlement out of court. Her lawyer, Hartley Dewart, K.C., prominent Liberal politician, who had had no chance of collecting fees for the defence of his client on the murder charge, jumped at this chance to make the Star Publishing Co. pay the shot. But it is doubtful if his cleverness paid off in the long run. Atkinson gave orders that Dewart's name was henceforth to be kept out of the *Star* newspapers, and politicians live on publicity.

Writing headings is a fine art. Not only must an editor use words which give a digest of, or create interest in, the story, but they must fit in a limited space. In searching for a word or phrase of the right length, there is always a risk of selecting one with a wrong shade of meaning.

On January 12, 1924, the *Star Weekly* began a series of articles by W. E. Raney, K.C., then Attorney-General of Ontario. It looked like a ten-strike to sign up the Attorney-General as a contributor but his first effort got us into trouble. In that article Raney quoted extensively from the Gregory Commission Report of April, 1922, on unsavoury police conditions in the city of Brantford. In his report, however, the commissioner had completely exonerated and recommended for another position Police Magistrate W. C. Livingston who had originally been dismissed.

One paragraph in the Raney article summarized what the Report had said of conditions in Brantford. A later paragraph told of a number of things which were known to Magistrate Livingston. It is customary for an editor to interpose at regular intervals through an article a number of sub-heads which are based on the reading matter immediately following.

I wrote a sub-head "All Known to Magistrate" to go above the second paragraph. This one line was the basis of a suit for $50,000 brought jointly against the *Star* and Raney. Magistrate Livingston's lawyer, W. S. Brewster, contended that the sub-head referred to everything in the article and that, since those words were not included in the Gregory report, they had been interpolated and were libelous.

They indicated, he argued, that the magistrate knew all, and was therefore inefficient and dishonest.

The case was tried before Justice Mowat, and J. M. McEvoy appeared for the *Star*.

Our defence was that the articles on law enforcement showed no malice or ill-feeling, but consisted of privileged matter and fair comment. The words "All Known to Magistrate" plainly referred only to matters in the following paragraph. No one expected to have a meticulously exact heading for every paragraph in a newspaper. The *Star* had subsequently printed that part of the report affirming Mr. Livingston's innocence. No witnesses were called for the defence.

Justice Mowat, in charging the jury, said that people wanted newspapers to be vigorous. They wanted strong meat which would lead to public discussion. There was a danger, however, that people would read only the headlines, and improper headlines could do injury. He considered the damages claimed, however, were "outrageous."

After three hours and fifteen minutes the jury brought in a verdict for the newspaper, with costs.

Commenting on the verdict, the *Star* declared editorially that this was the first time in twenty-five years that the paper had been in court in libel proceedings. It added:

No newspaper, particularly if it is alert and keen to gather and publish news that is interesting, can publish every day for twenty-five years amid the haste and pressure of modern newspaper conditions and not make mistakes. From time to time the *Star* has encountered complaints which it has endeavoured to meet in a spirit of fairness and sympathy, having in mind the principle that where wrong is done it should be righted. The contents of the article complained about were privileged material which a newspaper is entitled to print without exposing itself to a charge of libel.

Unfortunately for the *Star*, its lawyer and Raney had been too zealous in challenging prospective jurors. Politics were pretty hot in Brantford just then, and it was deemed Conservatives would be prejudiced against the *Star*. Altogether seven jurors were asked to step down and the legal limit was four.

An appeal was entered in the High Court of Ontario on this ground, and Magistrate Livingston was granted a new trial with costs.

When the new trial began Justice Mowat again presided. He declared it would be "a waste of time" to go over the whole thing again, and suggested the parties seek an out-of-court settlement. This was reached on the basis of the plaintiff withdrawing the record and consenting to have the action dismissed, and the defendants paying costs without in any way admitting liability for libel. I do not know exactly what it cost the *Star* but it was not a small sum.

My third libel case came years later when I was publisher of the weekly *Free Press Herald* at Midland. A reporter's story was printed concerning a woman of the community who, it was rumoured, was involved in a mysterious disappearance. The article stated that she could not be found, though "the police were normally well informed as to her whereabouts." The words quoted were held to constitute libel. We at first determined to fight the claim, and dug up a lot of material to support our statement. In the end, however, we decided it would be much cheaper to submit to what we considered blackmail than to go to court. The settlement, including legal costs, involved well over $1,000, a not inconsiderable sum for a country weekly. It would possibly have cost twice that to fight and win, as the plaintiff might not have been able to pay the costs.

Publishing a newspaper has other perils. There are always practical jokers, or folks who seek to vent spite by sending in innocent-looking personal paragraphs through the mail, such as "Mr. X spent the weekend with Mrs. Y at Port Smith." Of course, it may be quite all right. They may be brother and sister, but again they may not. Unless the editor knows the people, or that the information comes from a perfectly reliable source, he is wise to drop the item in the waste-paper basket. Such personal paragraphs are often packed with dynamite.

Three libel suits in fifty years is, however, not too bad. So perhaps I may be forgiven for blowing my own horn on a false report.

# 26 ⋘

## Crime Worse Than Murder

MY ONE AND ONLY associate editor on the *Star Weekly* was a man who had committed one of the worst crimes in the history of Canadian journalism—he had interviewed a Governor-General.

This is something in Canada which is just not done. Charlie Vining did it because neither he nor the Governor-General knew any better.

It happened just a year after Vining, as an eager young reporter, joined the staff of the Toronto *Daily Star* as a graduate from the University of Toronto. On his second out-of-town assignment he went to Quebec to report the arrival in Canada of Lord Byng. As he left the office, city editor Hindmarsh casually remarked that he might as well try to get an interview with Byng while he was at it.

"His remark was meant as a joke but I did not know it," Vining told me later. "When I got to Quebec I found that Byng's ship was docking late that afternoon with the ceremonial landing to take place in the morning. So I taxied down to the dock, walked aboard the almost deserted ship, located a young A.D.C. who was as innocent as I was, and presently found myself having a comfortable talk with Byng. He also was green, and he gave me a first rate interview, filled with war reminiscences, and ending up with a special message to the citizens of Toronto exclusively for the *Star*.

"I went back to the Chateau Frontenac, wrote my story which I was sure would be the main feature on the *Star's* front page the next day, and took it to the telegraph office.

"About half an hour later came a telephone call from Major Willis O'Connor, the Governor-General's senior A.D.C., who really knew the score. He was so filled with horror and indignation that he could scarcely speak, but he conveyed to me that I had committed a crime worse than murder in trapping Byng into breaking the sacred rule—the Governor-General *never* gives an interview to the press. If the story went out, he argued, Byng would likely be recalled; the Empire would crumble; and something awful would happen to me. Peremptorily he ordered me to go to the telegraph office, get my copy, and destroy it forthwith.

"I realized I must have got quite a story and, for once, I had presence of mind. When O'Connor stopped for breath I said: 'Sir, I think you are needlessly excited. No rule has been broken. I have not interviewed the Governor-General. I have only interviewed Lord Byng of Vimy. He will not become Governor-General until he is sworn in at noon tomorrow.'

"So the story ran in the *Star* next day, and with a by-line. And the local Quebec *Chronicle-Telegraph,* without permission, lifted the entire story and printed it as a front page feature—Special to the *Chronicle-Telegraph* by Charles Vining."

But Vining's glory was short-lived. While in Quebec, Charlie got a telegram from Bill Marchington, telegraph editor of the *Star,* telling him that a live turkey which he had won a few days before at a raffle in Penetanguishene while on his first out-of-town assignment, had been shipped to the *Star* and was at that moment in a crate in city editor Hindmarsh's office.

"I got an impression from Bill's wire that Hindmarsh did not appreciate this and that I had better do something, which I did," said Charlie.

Vining had been with the *Star* only a year when he was sent up to London to become managing editor of the London *Advertiser,* a dead horse which J. E. Atkinson had purchased in an ill-advised moment, believing that it might be the first in a string of Atkinson-owned papers. After four discouraging years trying to resuscitate the animal, Vining returned to Toronto as associate editor of the *Star Weekly.* I was delighted for he materially strengthened our staff.

Possessed of a keen, analytical mind as well as a flair both for descriptive writing and fun-making, Charlie's contribution added greatly to the *Star Weekly's* bill of fare. He was so good that I was not altogether surprised, though deeply disappointed, when the *Daily*

*Star* laid hands on him for special assignments all across Canada. Despite Atkinson's promise to relieve my growing administrative burden, no other associate editor was ever appointed.

One of Charlie Vining's more amusing feature stories on the *Star Weekly* centred around the native suspicion of Torontonians. One day I borrowed from the Canadian Bank of Commerce a $1,000 bill. These big bills were not then in general circulation, being used largely among the banks for the settlement of daily clearings. Giving the $1,000 bill to Charlie Vining and Greg Clark, I suggested that they go up Yonge Street through Toronto's major retail section and see what they could do with it in the shops. I suspected that when such a bill was presented in payment for a small article there might be repercussions which would make good story material.

Charlie and Greg first walked into a haberdashery. They picked out several ties, had them wrapped, accepted the parcel and then tendered the $1,000 bill. The clerk took one look at it and called for the manager. The latter studied the two customers carefully and then suggested that the ties be returned and the whole matter forgotten. Charlie and Greg protested vigorously the insult to their integrity, but to no avail. They had to return the ties and take back the bill.

When they next invaded a hosiery shop to buy some stockings for their wives, the proprietor threatened to call the police. Store after store flatly refused the $1,000 bill.

Tired of fooling around with the small fry the two pranksters headed into Eaton's big department store. Each picked out a handsome shirt and a couple of ties. They proferred the $1,000 bill. The clerk looked hard at it but did not blink. His not to reason why, his but to do and die. He put the big bill into the tube and shot it up to the cashier's office.

What happened up there none of us ever found out. Possibly the cashier phoned the bank. In any event, in a few minutes back came the change, $992 in fifties, twenties, tens, fives and a single two. The laugh was on Charlie and Greg. They had to stand there and count the wad of money while a wondering crowd gaped incredulously.

Their little adventure over, back they came to the office with the shirts and the ties and the $992. The money went back to the bank and perhaps the shirts and the ties went back to Eaton's. Or possibly the boys kept them as a reward for a stunt well performed.

Vining left the *Star* in 1928 while he was still young and full of energy. After some years at the Cockfield Brown Advertising Agency, he was appointed, in 1934, to the presidency of the Newsprint Association of Canada. During World War II he served for a time as assistant to the Chairman of the Wartime Prices and Trade Board, and later Chairman of the government's Wartime Information Board.

If interviewing a Governor-General is a journalistic crime, Charlie Vining is living proof that at least occasionally crime does pay.

# 27 ⋘

## *His Hero Was a Matador*

ONE DAY, just a little more than a year after the end of the First World War, Gregory Clark brought a stranger to my door.

He was a tall, slim, loose-jointed lad with flushed cheeks, glowing black eyes, a thick black moustache and untidy black hair surmounting a round face. He wore a peaked cap, a leather coat short in the arms, and tight grey trousers that were slightly "highwater." He walked with a slight limp.

"Boss," said Greg, "this fellow says he can write, and he wants to do something for us."

The stranger stood while he talked to me. He told me he was an American, then visiting at the home of Ralph Connable, well-to-do manager of Woolworths in Toronto. He had quit school; vagabonded around the United States riding the rods and sleeping in tramp jungles; but, when war broke out, had gone with an American volunteer ambulance unit to Italy, later transferring to active service with the famous Italian Arditi regiment.

Our interview was very matter of fact. Yes, he had done a little work as a cub reporter on the Kansas City *Star*, under whose auspices the ambulance unit went overseas. So I asked him to submit something on approval. His first effort, an article about paintings circulating from home to home, was published in the *Weekly's* magazine section on February 14, 1920. There was nothing unusual about it; just the sort of thing any good cub reporter could turn out. He got $5 for the 1,000 words.

His next article, written in terse, short paragraphs, and laced with humour, dealt with the free shaves offered by the Toronto barber college, where students learned their trade by practising on courageous or penniless volunteers.

He told how he noticed the heavily bandaged left hand of the apprentice who was lathering his face.

"How did you do that?" he asked.

"Damn near slashed my thumb off with a razor this morning," the student replied amiably.

"The shave was not all," he recorded. "Scientists say that hanging is a very pleasant death. The pressure of the rope on the nerves and arteries produces a sort of anaesthesia. It is waiting to be hanged that bothers a man."

From that time on, our American friend was a more or less regular contributor on a space basis. He was paid half a cent a word, our regular rate on the *Star Weekly* in those early days.

He used to come into the office and sit on the radiator, talking and interrupting the work of the staff. He was a good talker and, like Greg Clark, would much rather talk than sit down to work at a typewriter.

Sometimes I listened in. I remember being fascinated by the stories of his adventures in eating. He was ready to try anything once —slugs, earthworms, snails, ants.

One day Greg told me that this adventurer of ours was writing a book with a funny name—*The Sun Also Rises*. He said he had seen some pages of it and was not much impressed. The style was curious, jerky and machine-gun-like. I suggested that Greg should not discourage the lad. Lots of young fellows were trying to write books and some of them succeeded.

Altogether that year our new contributor wrote twenty-four pieces for the *Star Weekly* and he was around the office so much we came to look on him almost as a member of the permanent staff.

In 1921 he continued to submit short articles and also contributed occasionally to the *Daily Star*. But more and more time went to his books. Moreover he was married in September for the first time and, with the former Elizabeth Hadley Richardson, spent the early part of the winter in Chicago.

In December of that year he went to Europe as a roving correspondent for the *Daily Star*, covering in 1922 the World Economic Conference at Genoa and the Lausanne Conference, following the Turkish Army across Macedonia, and becoming a bull fight fan in Spain. His first son, born on October 10, 1923, in Toronto, was Nicanor, named after the great Spanish matador of that day, Nicanor Vallalta.

Back in Toronto in the autumn of that year, and living in a sparsely furnished apartment in the north of the city, he joined the home staff of the *Daily Star*. One of his major assignments was to meet the former British Prime Minister, Lloyd George, in New York City and accompany him and his daughter, Megan, on a tour across Canada. He also wrote one or more pieces a week for me, some of them under the pen name of John Hadley, the last half of which he borrowed from his wife's maiden name.

Many stories have been told as to why he finally left the *Star*. One of these, obviously untrue, was that he had been fired by city editor Hindmarsh "because he could not write." Another had it that he balked at being given the job of advance agent for a white peacock, which was being presented as a publicity stunt by the *Star* to the Toronto Zoo. It was alleged that his resignation, ten yards of copy paper in length, had been pasted to the bulletin board in the news room.

My own recollection is that he resigned after a series of clashes with city editor Hindmarsh. Managing editor John Bone had brought him home to be a first line reporter with the *Daily Star* after he had won prestige for his European articles. The *Star's* city editor then gave him the standard treatment for reducing prima donnas to size. Once, after working until midnight on a major story, he was called out of bed at 4.30 a.m. to cover an unimportant fire. Thereafter, he was given a series of other minor assignments designed, apparently, to humiliate and exasperate.

One day he had breakfast with an Hungarian diplomat, Count Apponyi, whose address that noon to a city club he was to report. The diplomat lent him some important papers regarding Hungarian aspirations on the understanding that they were to be returned when his story was completed. He sent the papers by messenger with an explanatory note to city editor Hindmarsh but, when he later came back to the office to get them, he discovered they had been thrown in the waste-paper basket and could not be found. Whereupon he blew up and resigned.

Hindmarsh, however, has another version. He says that the famed European correspondent was simply "too big for his breeches," and would not conform to *Star* standards and directions. Sent to northern Ontario to cover a labour dispute, his despatches so favoured the strikers that Hindmarsh had to wire him to start reporting the news. Whereupon he is said to have returned to Toronto and, after expressing somewhat heatedly his opinion of the city editor, to have handed in his resignation.

In any event when, some years after he left the *Star,* the Toronto Newspaper Guild was fighting for recognition as the bargaining agent for the newspaper's editorial employees, he wrote the Guild saying he was enclosing $100 "to beat Hindmarsh." After expressing his dislike of his old boss, he added, "on second thought I am making it $200."

No matter what the true facts were, when the resignation took effect, he came to see me, said he had decided to go back to Paris, and asked if he could write a series of articles for the *Star Weekly* in return for sufficient money to buy his rail and steamship tickets. Managing Editor Bone O.K.'d the arrangement.

Recently I had a letter from Greg Clark's stranger, his hair now grown grey. He gave me permission to quote from it only these three sentences. "I never enjoyed myself so much as working under you and with Greg Clark and Jimmy Frise. It was why I was sad to quit newspaper work. Working under the other fellow was like being in the German army with a poor commander."

So his three years on the Toronto *Star* were described by Ernest Hemingway.

# 28 «««

## Fired From Every Job

WORLD FAMOUS NOVELIST and reporter Ernest Hemingway may have been one of the best known writers to have parted company with the *Star,* but he couldn't compare his record with that of Gordon Sinclair.

If parting is "such sweet sorrow," Gordon would have been able to swim in saccharin tears. He was fired eleven times from the *Star* and had his salary reduced five times, once as much as forty per cent.

"But," he told me, "I had a lot of fun and I don't think they got me down." He was with the *Star* off and on for a total of about twenty-one years, and even now he is writing a radio feature for the *Daily.* They just do not seem to be able to get along without him.

On one occasion, *Star* editor Hindmarsh handed him $5,000 and told him to "get out and stay out." Yet six years later, the same Hindmarsh invited Gordon to fly around the world at *Star* expense by any route he chose and tell *Star* readers about what he saw. And this was only one of the four globe-circling journalistic assignments, and twenty-three foreign journeys, which have made his adventures worthy of inclusion in a modern Arabian Nights.

It is not only his travelling expenses which have cost his publishers money. Sinclair has been co-defendant in libel suits to the tune of $120,000, and has lost every action by out-of-court settlement. In each case the money was paid by the *Star.* "And I never so much as received a reprimand," says Gordon.

By orthodox newspaper standards, Sinclair is not a great reporter. He breaks all the rules. His news broadcasts differ from most in that he gives his own slant to events. His language is decidedly earthy at times but he gets away with it. Anything that comes into his head is likely to come out his mouth, literally anything. President Harry

Sedgewick of radio station CFRB once said that Sinclair gets them into more controversies than all other newscasters combined. Yet the public likes his stuff.

Money and Gordon Sinclair have been friends for many years and they are likely to stick together for some time yet. Now that he has become a top-flight radio commentator, his earnings are among the highest in the publicity business. And he is one of the very few journalists of my acquaintance who claims to be able to write a cheque for $100,000 which won't bounce.

Sinclair was born and educated in Toronto, and as a youth tried his hand successively, if not altogether successfully, at banking, book-keeping, and selling perfume, calendars and ties. "I have been fired from every job I ever held," he confesses cheerfully. While working in Eaton's, he had the unusual experience of selling a necktie to Sir John Eaton himself. He wrote a little piece about it and sent it to the *Star Weekly*. The story was accepted, and Sinclair was paid $3. This started him on his writing career. Other stories were accepted and in course of time Gordon joined the *Daily Star* as a reporter.

On my library shelf is a copy of Sinclair's book *Footloose in India*. Its flyleaf bears, over Gordon's signature, the inscription: "He gave me encouragement when I needed it." This is a reference to my purchase of his first article for the *Star Weekly*.

For a while, Sinclair worked hard as a cub reporter, doing the usual run of routine assignments. Then came his big chance. It was 1929, the year of the financial crash, and, as a byproduct of hard times, a "hobo jungle" had sprung up on the outskirts of Toronto. The police ordered the jobless men to leave town. Sinclair was assigned by the *Star* to join the trek and write what he saw. Three days later he got into a fight with a sailor and received a gash over one eye. He returned to Toronto and reported that nothing of interest had happened. He was told to write something anyway, and his copy proved so unusual that Hindmarsh sent him back after the hoboes with instructions to follow them to England where they said they were going. Gordon never found them but he did go to England, and thus began a series of travel tales for the *Star* that established Sinclair as a "wandering reporter" of unique gifts.

People sometimes wondered how much was fact, and how much fiction, in Gordon's travel stories. After his return from India, I invited him to give a talk to some friends in my home. A guest was dubious about Gordon having actually plunged into the sacred Ganges for a swim, so I asked him about it. "Well, the *Star* had to have a good story," was the evasive reply. But city editor Gerald Brown of the *Star* once paid tribute to him in these words: "I should like to vouch for his astonishing accuracy. Sinclair sees events through a special pair of eyes. He has a rare nose for adventure. Things happen when Sinclair is around."

Then there was the famous story of the Vanderbilt lion hunt. As it appeared in the *Star* under Sinclair's name, the tale told how George Vanderbilt, millionaire game hunter, had caught lions in Africa by dragging behind his speeding car shark and tarpon hooks baited with zebra meat. Lions were declared to be "the bunk." "They are getting so denatured and devitalized in the African pampas that you can get out and chase them," Vanderbilt was quoted as saying.

It is quite possible that Vanderbilt told the story to Gordon just as he wrote it. Men sometimes kid reporters for fun, and Gordon undoubtedly set the tale down as he heard it, also for fun.

When the yarn was printed, however, it caused a continent-wide outburst of protests. Vanderbilt declared that neither he nor his party had hunted lions in the manner described. He alleged that Sinclair had misinterpreted what he had said about the methods used in getting first class motion pictures of lions by dragging zebra meat behind the car. The meat was tied to a rope. The lions smelled it and galloped after it while the cameras clicked.

Vanderbilt entered suit for heavy damages against the *Star*. In its published defence the paper said that this was the first occasion on which any correction of Sinclair's statements had become necessary. It explained that Gordon had recently been ill with malaria, which probably accounted for his error of hearing. The libel suit was settled out of court.

But despite his usual association with hair-raising adventure yarns, Gordon was at one time editor of the *Star's* Woman's Page. Most of us thought he had been sent there for punishment. He says not, and here is his own story.

There had been two or three women writing the society news, weddings, etc. but Mrs. Atkinson apparently got the idea that these women were a menace around the paper and orders were given that they were to be dropped. Clifford Wallace was put in charge. He was promptly renamed "Nellie" by the other guys. He couldn't take the ribbing so they turned the job over to me. Presumably because I had a much thicker skin.

From the beginning I never took the job seriously, expecting I would either be fired or soon moved to other work. As a consequence I used to come in at eight in the morning and, except on Saturdays, quit for the day about eleven. I shamelessly clipped most of my material from other newspapers, and stuck to the job for about fourteen months until young Joe Atkinson, who was at that time a proof reader, noticed that all my stuff had previously been published in some other paper. So I was eventually sent back to the news room, and Helen MacMillan was brought down from London to take over the Woman's Page.

Gordon also served a term as sports editor after Lou Marsh's death. One would have thought that his breezy style would go well, but somehow he did not hit it off. He just was not interested enough in sports.

When Sinclair accepted an invitation to tell of his travel experiences on the radio, J. E. Atkinson objected, and issued an order that no *Star* man was to take on broadcasting engagements. In 1939 Sinclair and Matthew Halton decided to put the ban to a test. At the end of three months they both got an order to quit radio or quit the newspaper. Both resigned.

But today Sinclair is one of radio's most popular newscasters, and he is still writing for the *Star*.

# 29 ⋘

## No Particular Fool Himself

WHEN I WAS SEVENTEEN years old, my hero was the minister of Galt's Knox Church—the Reverend Robert E. Knowles.

Coming to my home town and home church from Stewarton Presbyterian in Ottawa, he was a young man of unusual oratorical gifts. Irish by descent and temperament, blessed with a picturesquely poetic vocabulary, well read and a superb story teller, he also possessed a fine flow of wit. Morning and evening he swayed at will the congregations which packed the big church. No pulpit confined him. He strode back and forth preaching passionately the gospel of a Christ who desired the souls of men. I never missed a service.

When I went to Woodstock and joined Knox Church there I urged the aged minister, Rev. Dr. McMullen, to invite Mr. Knowles to exchange pulpits for a Sunday. He did so.

Dr. McMullen was a quiet man. He ended his sermon with every hair in place and his clothing faultless. But when Knowles donned the doctor's gown, it was soon evident that trouble was brewing. The clerical tabs below his chin were loose and, the more he warmed to his subject, the more they flapped in his face. Suddenly, his eyes flashing, Knowles grabbed the offending tabs and, with a rip that could be heard in the farthest corner of the church, tore them from their moorings. Never shall I forget the wave first of shocked amazement and then amusement which swept over the temporarily scandalized congregation. Knowles was not invited back to Woodstock.

I remember another incident in Knowles' preaching career which he himself loved to recount. When occupying the pulpit in a distant city, the soprano soloist came to him before the service and said: "Mr. Knowles, I will be singing right after your sermon. If you will tell me your subject, I will select an appropriate solo."

"Well, really, I hardly think I can—," he stammered. "That is, I . . ."

"Never mind," she interrupted. "I will listen carefully and, before you are finished, I will select something suitable."

It was a long sermon and one which the congregation found rather difficult to follow. When Knowles sat down, the soprano rose and sang: "Some Day We'll Understand."

For the first eight years of his pastorate at Knox, Galt, Knowles preached with success and the church prospered. Then, in 1905, some of the kirk's elders were greatly disturbed. Who could have foreseen that their minister would write "sic an unco wicked thing"? The Reverend Robert Knowles had published *St. Cuthbert's*, his first novel. Reviewers hailed him as Canada's "Ian Maclaren." Everybody, including the elders who held that any novel was a work of Satan, read it. *St. Cuthbert's* was readily recognizable as their own Knox kirk, and some of its characters resembled mightily the pillars of the church. Knowles in his years at Galt had made himself the master of the Scottish dialect spoken by so many of his flock, and never was a book devoured more thoroughly by a whole community.

Not only did the novel do well in Galt. It was a Canadian best seller. His publishers demanded more, and there appeared at regular intervals: *The Web of Time, The Undertow, The Dawn at Shanty Bay,* and *The Attic Guest,* the last named telling the story of his own courtship of and marriage to a Southern belle.

As a novelist Knowles portrayed a rugged, honest and God-fearing people. Laughter and tears were always close together. And, in addition to his novels, he began each year to cover the Presbyterian General Assemblies for the Toronto *Globe*.

But suddenly, at the height of his church and book-writing fame, he was badly hurt in a railway accident near Georgetown, Ontario. The man sitting beside him was killed, and Knowles, himself, suffered a badly broken shoulder blade. After months in hospital he went back to his work in Galt, but could not carry on. His damaged nerves made it impossible either to write or preach. He resigned his pulpit, collapsed completely, and was confined to hospital in Toronto for psychiatric treatment.

In the summer of 1921, I received word that he had been discharged from hospital and would like to see me. Although white and drawn, and shrinking from contact with unfamiliar people, he told me he wanted a chance to prove himself by writing. I encouraged him to try. His "Indiscretions of the Great" I published in the *Star Weekly*.

It was some weeks before he wrote again. Then, as he gained in health and confidence, his articles appeared with more regularity. For a year we had two articles a week from his pen. Our readers liked them. So did Atkinson. I was not surprised when the *Daily Star* asked him to accept regular assignments, and turned him loose on his interviewing career.

Knowles' interviews were decidedly different. One could never be sure how much was Knowles and how much the person interviewed. In *Star* tradition, he was more intent on entertaining than on informing his readers. And while the so-called intelligentsia loathed his stories, most readers loved them.

To be interviewed by R. E. Knowles was a novel experience for celebrities who came to Toronto. Those who appreciated daring and witty repartee liked him and liked his methods. The sober-minded wished he would quit fooling and get down to business. The ladies, according to "R. E. K." himself, literally ate up his flattering appraisals of their beauty and charm, and his oft repeated assertions that their voices were like "chimes of bells."

One prominent Canadian said to me: "I did not know whether I was being interviewed by Knowles, or whether I was interviewing him. When the story was printed, there was more of Knowles in it than there was of me. However, it was mighty well done."

R. E. Knowles had his own formula for successful interviewing. This is how he described it to the members of the Toronto Women's Press Club:

The first essential of an interviewer is to have a fine opinion of oneself. It is necessary to so vary oneself, so to control and direct one's speech, that great men realize that you are no particular fool yourself. There is no such joy to the interviewee as to find a man of magnitude interviewing him. It is fatal to exhibit or cherish an inferiority complex.

He was absolutely right. Interviewing is a fine art and should never be trusted to the ill-informed and incompetent. A well-trained reporter who is assigned to interview a celebrity will, if he is wise and has time, read everything he can find on the man or woman with whom he is to talk. He will seek to understand what most interests that person. Nothing so annoys a person being interviewed as to discover that the reporter knows little or nothing of the subject under discussion, and he will generally shut up like a clam.

A well-read, well-informed reporter, who, to quote Knowles' words, is "no particular fool himself," can generally carry off an interview successfully even with a person who does not want to talk. Most

public men have suffered so at the hands of the press that, when a
competent journalist appears, a worth-while interview results. Often
the person interviewed will take the trouble to give such a reporter
an "off the record" background which will enable him to handle the
subject with wisdom, and write an accurate informative story without
revealing the source.

Here is part of a typical Knowles interview with a woman
celebrity:

Elizabeth Arden is a world famed person. For the first time in my
life I met this morning a lady who has made herself a millionairess
. . . which is a much more wonderful creation than a mere million
heiress. She received me most graciously and I could not but begin
with:

"Miss Arden, it is delightful to observe that one who preaches the
duty of feminine beauty practises what she preaches."

"Awfully sweet of you," quoth she, "but to be quite frank I have
always considered myself plain—but I have always claimed, for all
that, that I can make anybody beautiful."

"As a philosopheress, Miss Arden, please tell me, is the old proverb
that beauty is only skin deep a true one?"

"No, it is false. No supreme beauty can be acquired without the
aid of the soul. After all the heart is beauty's great fountainhead and
hiding place," pronounced the thoughtful Miss Arden.

"Do you approve of magenta or crushed strawberry finger nails?"

"No, I don't." And that was distinctly that.

"I have had cases where their own husbands failed, after the
improvements, to recognize their own wives," she went on.

"Probably quite a relief in many cases," I surmised. "Is the love
of beauty in a woman's mysterious heart instinctive or implanted?"

"It should be instinctive but it can be implanted too."

"Can beauty in a woman come to pass without the aid of
cosmetics?"

"No, sooner or later through the all-devouring years, beauty
becomes only a memory without proper aid."

"Now a real question," I foreadvised. "Tell me, O tell me the
truth. Is there such a thing as kiss-proof lipstick?"

"Yes," was the calm reply, "but it all depends upon the way in
which it is put on."

"I would like to see it demonstrated," I said, looking into the
fine eyes with childlike innocence, hoping for a sympathetic interpretation of my quest for knowledge—but, all indifferent, Miss Arden
went on: "I have often been asked if cosmetics permit sea bathing
or rather survive it, and my reply is a simple 'Never'."

There were some things which even an interviewer like R. E.
Knowles couldn't extract from a woman!

# 30 ≪≪←

## *The Indian Sign*

IT WAS IN 1923 that I bought for the *Star Weekly* the first of a series of articles by one of the most colourful writers ever to come out of the Canadian West.

And when Chief Buffalo Child Long Lance shot himself on March 20, 1932, in the California home of the daughter of mining magnate "Lucky" Baldwin, the bullet ended not only a close personal friendship but a career unmatched by that of any Canadian Indian of the present century.

The tragedy went unexplained. An Associated Press despatch merely said that he had been drinking heavily. No inquest was held.

Long Lance was a chief of the Blood tribe of Alberta, one of the four principal tribes of the Northern Blackfeet. His father, Mountain Horse, was a chief when buffalo still roamed the prairies. His own earliest recollections were of the piercing yells from the big round lodge where the braves of the tribe were enduring the tortures of the Sun Dance. Riding, hunting, shooting, roving filled his youth. At fourteen, when he rode down with others of his tribe to participate in the Frontier Day celebrations at Cheyenne, Wyoming, he joined Buffalo Bill's Wild West Show for a tour of the United States. He saw the white man for the first time in a civilized environment and said to himself: "I'm going to be like that."

Long Lance enrolled in 1909 at the famous Carlisle Indian School, graduating three years later as valedictorian and senior honour graduate, captain of the cavalry troup, president of the literary society, member of the debating team, vice-president of the student government, president of the Y.M.C.A., treasurer of the senior class, and first clarionet in the school band.

Blessed with a magnificent body, he was a member of the famous Carlisle Indian rugby team when Jim Thorpe, the greatest all-round athlete of all time, was its captain. In the Olympic trials, Long Lance bested Thorpe three times in the mile. Jack Dempsey, who himself had a streak of Indian blood, and Long Lance were close friends. "Chief," Dempsey once said to him, "if I had you for three months I could make you light heavyweight boxing champion of the world." Long Lance did win the light heavyweight title of the Canadian Army in the First World War and, despite the fact that he gave away over fifty pounds, four times threw Frank Leavitt, heavyweight wrestling champion of the United States army.

Leaving Carlisle, Long Lance was for a year at Dickinson College, where he won a scholarship to St. John's Military Academy at Manlius, N.Y. There he added both to his athletic and scholastic distinctions and, on graduation, President Woodrow Wilson personally nominated him for appointment to West Point, the first Indian ever chosen to be an American army officer.

But Long Lance did an extraordinary thing. He threw up his appointment, came home to Canada, and, in a Calgary recruiting office, enlisted as a private in a battalion of the American Legion. He left for overseas with the 97th one week after putting on uniform.

Drafted to the 38th battalion, he became sniping and scouting sergeant and later sergeant-major. He was commissioned on the field and rose to a captaincy of Calgary's 50th battalion, winning the Croix de Guerre for gallantry and devotion to duty. He was twice severely wounded and only his magnificent physique saved him from a double amputation.

For a year following World War I, Long Lance was in the intelligence department of the general staff and, on the recommendation of General Biddle, commander-in-chief of U.S. troops in Britain, was offered a captaincy in the American permanent force. But he refused, came back to Canada, and decided to seek a career in journalism.

He joined the Calgary *Herald* and won his spurs on every beat from police to city hall to sports. He made a name for himself not as an Indian but as a first rate writer. But a practical joke ended his career on the *Herald*. He was assigned one night to what proved to be a very dull session of the municipal council. Thoroughly bored, Long Lance slipped quietly out of the chambers and, following a hunt through the nearby police offices, fashioned a "bomb" out of a black rubber ball filled with sawdust but equipped with a live fuse. When the city fathers became aware of the sputtering "bomb" which he had placed beneath their council table, a near riot ensued. They fled en masse for the nearest exits. One city commissioner crashed head foremost through a closed window and fell into a snowbank below. Another commissioner, too fat to follow, stuck in the window. The next day the whole city rocked with laughter. But the *Herald* fired its red-blooded scribe. The mayor and city commissioners, themselves, sought to intervene on his behalf. So did a deputation of Calgary business men. Bob Edwards, famous editor of the Calgary *Eye Opener,* termed it "the best joke ever pulled off in Western Canada," and protested the dismissal. But all to no avail.

So that city lost the man who had had much to do with the organization of its famous Calgary Stampede and who, in his native costume, had been one of the Stampede's star performers; and the Canadian Pacific Railway, the amazing Indian who had acted as host when celebrities visited its Banff and other Rocky Mountain resorts.

Not long before, Long Lance had been made a chief of the Blood tribe of Alberta's Blackfeet. The chieftain's bonnet of feathers had been placed on his head by his father, Mountain Horse, and he had been given the name of a famous Indian warrior of the past, "Buffalo Child." His father had told him: "Always seek to be the great Indian whose spirit now comes back to earth and enters your body."

Chief Buffalo Child Long Lance once more began to rove. He did a series of articles on the Indian tribes of the West Coast for the Vancouver *Sun,* and the following year a similar series on the Indians of the prairies for the Regina *Leader.* Then for a brief period he was on the reportorial staff of the Winnipeg *Tribune.*

His first article for me was the story of a Canadian Sioux Chief, and, not long after, he was a top-drawer writer in both Canadian and United States newspapers and magazines. Not once in the nine years I knew him did he ever turn in a poor story.

Each time he came to Toronto he was a visitor at our home. A great favourite with our boys, he would run upstairs to their room as soon as he came, and would sit on the floor with them, spinning Indian stories. An unusual conversationalist, he was completely at ease in any field and his talk sparkled with humour. His autobiography, *Long Lance,* published in New York in 1928, has a foreword by his close friend Irvin S. Cobb.

Long Lance was tall, slim and well-built, lithe in movement and quick in speech, with a handsome face and a brilliant intellect. Only his high cheek bones and straight black hair suggested Indian blood. He was lionized by fellow-writers and by literary hangers-on, both male and female. Wealthy women invited him to their homes. He felt he was accepted by them as an equal and dreamed of marrying a white girl.

More than once he had discussed this marriage problem with me. With all earnestness I urged that he seek out and marry a cultured girl of his own race. His most respected Indian professor at Carlisle had also warned him that marriage to a white woman would bring only disappointment and unhappiness.

Long Lance told me that if he married a white girl he would be forever disowned by his fellow Indians. He was tremendously proud of his descent and colour. Despite his acceptance in the white man's world, he never forgot he was an Indian. His tribal brothers, however, progressively turned against him because they felt he had deserted his own people. As a renegade they gave him a cold reception on his trips back to the reservation at Cardston.

Yet this leader of North American Indians, one of the most brilliant writers I have ever published, a man at the peak of his career and in the prime of life, tripped over a racial hurdle and killed himself. He had perhaps forgotten the last paragraph of the last chapter of his own book:

... the new day is here: it is here to stay. And now we must leave it to our old people to sit solidly and dream of the glories of our past. Our job is to fit ourselves into the new scheme of life which the Great Spirit has decreed for North America. And we will do that, keeping always before us the old Blackfoot proverb: Mokokit-ki-ackamimat— Be wise and persevere.

# 31 ⋘

## *The Poet Died*

JUST TWO MONTHS before Long Lance committed suicide, another friend of *Star Weekly* days had died in Vancouver.

This is his story—in one chapter, although he really deserves a book.

One day, in that unbelievable year before the First World War, as I worked at my editorial desk I became conscious of shuffling footsteps and a strong smell of unwashed humanity. I looked up and there stood one of the most dismal looking derelicts I had ever seen.

His clothes were ragged and filthy, and red-rimmed eyes peered at me out of a haggard face covered with black smudges. He smelt strongly of whiskey.

"Could I sell you a poem?"

A grimy hand, projecting six inches beyond the sleeve of a verminous-looking overcoat, held out an even grimier piece of paper.

Ordinarily I would have said, "No, thank you. We don't buy poetry." But something about him compelled my interest. Possibly it was the cultured English voice. Perhaps it was the incongruity of poetry being offered by a drunken derelict. Possibly it was an Unseen Power which had brought two human beings together for a purpose.

I looked at the verses and was struck by their musical phrasing. I asked if they were his own work.

"Yes, I wrote it. Will you buy it? I must have some food."

"And why," I asked, "are you who possess such a gift from God, why are you as you are?" For a moment there was no answer. Then: "She died."

That was all he ever told me. Though we became intimate friends, I never learned whether the "she" was mother, sister, sweetheart, or wife. But after her death he had taken to drink, and sunk lower and lower till he touched the depths.

His name was Eric Ross Goulding, and he came of an aristocratic English family. He had taught in an English public school, spent some years in the Indian civil service, and fought in the Boer War as a cavalryman. Then he had made his bed in hell.

I bought the poem, and for a time he came back each day with others. I could not buy them all, but he had enough money for food.

Then he disappeared. A few weeks later a letter came from Fonthill, with more poems. He was working as a farm labourer. I then did what I had lacked the courage to do before. I wrote and told him about Jesus Christ and that I was praying for him. We prayed together, he in Fonthill and I in Toronto.

The miracle happened. He stopped drinking, and his letters were full of happiness. Six months passed and I got him a job in Toronto. He arrived in the city, drunk. We prayed together and he sobered up. I outfitted him with new clothes and a walking stick—the latter his own idea. He said it helped his morale. For three or four months he worked at his job and left alcohol alone. He was at our house almost every day; he still needed encouragement. And we enjoyed his company. He had travelled widely, was well versed in literature and politics, was a delightful conversationalist, and a most handsome young man.

Then he slipped, and lost his job. He climbed back on the wagon and made a new start. A friend got him a job at the Ontario parliament buildings. For a time he did well but he could not stand the confinement. He would go out for lunch, and wander among the trees and flowers all afternoon. When he was let out, he left the city without telling me, ashamed of his failure.

Months later, I learned he had shipped on a lake boat and then got a job with an American road gang. When war came, he returned to Canada, went overseas with the Royal Canadian Regiment, and, in the battle of Courcelette, had half his face shot off.

They patched him up in an English hospital. He wrote me occasionally, declaring that he was so horrible to look at that he would never let me see him again.

When I next heard of him, he was in Vancouver, writing poems, essays, and even editorials for the local press. I learned from a newspaper friend that Eric, though his physical condition did not permit his holding a regular job, was supporting himself by his pen, and was never known to take a drink.

One day in January, 1932, Eric Goulding collapsed in a Vancouver restaurant, and died in a military hospital. His tired heart had quit. The Vancouver papers, for all of which he had written, printed tributes to the man whose work had been an inspiration to so many people.

As I think back now to that day in 1913 when first we met, and the transformation which followed, I remember his lyric "Immortality."

> A poet dreamed and, dreaming, made a song.
> Men laughed the poet and his dream to scorn.
> The poet, dreaming, went his way along,
>     Neglected and forlorn.
>
> Then came a man of wealth and vast repute—
> Yea, one who had reached world eminence—
> Dazzling the throng which stood amazed and mute
>     And filled with reverence.
>
> The rich man died, and with him too, his fame;
> Nought had he done to cheer the toiler's way;
> The poet died, but men recall his name
>     And sing his songs today.

# 32 «««

## Two Big Little Men

TWO OF THE most courageous contributors which the *Star* ever boasted were men whose bodies were weak to the point of frailty.

Both were social reformers—Salem Bland, a Methodist minister, badgered from his professorial chair and his pulpit because of radical beliefs; Henry Somerville, an ardent Roman Catholic who put principle before policy, and traded his job as the *Star's* representative in London, England, for the editorship of Toronto's *Canadian Register*.

Physically, Dr. Salem Bland was a cripple. He was short, his back bent. A cane supported his weak legs. His skin was transparently white. He looked as though a little breeze would blow him over. Yet he had an unconquerable spirit and unmovable convictions. So sincerely did he love his fellow men that, on their behalf, he was ready to make any sacrifice.

When first I heard his name he was professor of church history and New Testament exegesis at Winnipeg's Wesley College. He had won fame as a preacher and was idolized by his students in no small part because of his radical views on economics and politics. He was an out-and-out socialist who believed that only through the nationalization of all industry could the rights of the common man be secured.

Because he persisted in publicly backing the rising labour unions in their bid for better wages and working conditions, Dr. Bland antagonized business leaders in the Methodist Church. When he refused to stop teaching and preaching that the Kingdom of God should come in this world, and that the working man was entitled to a larger share of the wealth he produced, they demanded his resignation. The board of governors capitulated and Salem Bland was out of a job.

For two years he remained in Winnipeg, making frequent labour speeches. When he dared to criticize the quality of the food supplied to Canadian soldiers in the First World War, he was called before the bar of the House of Commons.

Then he came to Toronto as minister of Broadway Methodist Tabernacle. It was not long before he was again in trouble with the well-to-do members of the congregation. He tendered his resignation, but the majority of the church people refused to accept it. However, when he later began to denounce fundamentalists for putting chains on religious liberty, and to argue that there was a considerable human element in the Scriptures, the congregation split. When the ministerial posts were next assigned by the stationing committee, Dr. Bland was left without a charge.

Even that did not muzzle him. He accepted a call from the Western Congregational Church, near by his former Methodist Tabernacle on Spadina Avenue. There he had a free pulpit and he spoke his mind without interference until his retirement.

It was about the time of his last pastoral shift that I first met him. I can recall with what amazement I looked upon this five-foot Lion of Judah, this fearless champion of the underdog who had defied millionaires. Was this the mighty man who had stood against the hurricanes of privilege and power?

He began to write a regular column, "The Observer," for the *Daily Star*, and I published an article from his pen in each issue of the *Weekly*.

In his earlier years, Dr. Bland had been a sincere believer in the Russian experiment, but became disillusioned when he saw that communism was based on materialism alone and that it had no place for God. Salem Bland was never, himself, a communist, but he did believe in a Christian socialist state, and many of the things for which he fought became realities. When, in February, 1950, at the age of ninety, he left this world, he left it a better place.

\* \* \* \* \*

In 1933, when Henry Somerville published in London, England, his book *The Catholic Social Movement*, he sent me a copy inscribed with the following words: "Knowing that you have many autographed books from your literary godchildren, you may be interested in this from a brother victim."

The joint victimization referred to the fact that in the previous year he, like many others before him, had been fired by the *Star* and, by 1933, I had also severed my connections with the newspaper that had been my journalistic home for twenty-nine years. But more of that anon.

Somerville was physically a bird-like man but one whose spirit soared the skies of literature, philosophy, history and economics. Secretary and one of the principal organizers of the Catholic Social Guild at Oxford University, he had won high scholastic honours at Ruskin College and, as an editor of the *Manchester Guardian,* was well known and respected in British journalism.

Coming to Canada after the First World War, he had joined the Toronto reportorial staff of the *Star* under managing editor John Bone, but was soon sent back to London as the *Star's* overseas correspondent. His despatches were informative, reliable, and written with great clarity. He was proud both of his job and his opportunity to serve as an interpreter to Canada of his native land. In an article which he wrote in 1927 for *T.P.-Cassell's Weekly,* Somerville described his work in these terms:

News agencies can give a more complete and rapid service than any number of correspondents, but they cannot be efficient interpreters. They have to cater to many papers of different types, and must be colourless and neutral. The correspondent, being primarily an interpreter of news which is current history, must understand the psychology of two nations, the one he writes about and the one he writes for. In the duplication of his sympathies and interests he must almost be two men in one.

If the London correspondent of a great overseas newspaper is the right man, he has the most fascinating and enviable job in the whole realm of journalism. The big news of the day is always his assignment. If it is an important debate, he is at the House of Commons. If there is a big legal action on, he is at the High Courts. If there is a royal garden party, he is at Buckingham Palace. If there is an international crisis, he is at the Foreign Office. A representative of an English home paper is but a cog in a wheel. The London correspondent is a newspaper personality in himself. He receives the deference and the privileges due to the accredited representative of another nation.

It was in June, 1932, that Henry Somerville left the *Star.* In a letter which I received from him some time later he described, as follows, the series of events which led to his ousting:

That week I had received a very cordial letter from *Daily Star* managing editor Hindmarsh asking me to do a bit of investigation of Mrs. Atkinson's family tree. I had been in Carmarthen, Wales, for two days tracing the family of Thomas Culham and Ann Evans who were married in the eighteenth century and were ancestors of Mrs. Atkinson. I came home to find the note of dismissal. Hindmarsh said he had come to the conclusion that I was "not in sympathy with the type of journalism which the *Star* is trying to develop."

While my dismissal came as a bolt from the blue, I had long been thinking that I would be forced to quit the job. The stuff that had been wanted was such that I could not supply it and retain my self respect. Many of the subjects were largely fakes—haunted castles, family curses, clan feuds, long lost heirs claiming fabulous fortunes, and gangsters in London.

Nonetheless my sense of humour was somehow tickled at having to reply to Hindmarsh simultaneously on the pedigree of his mother-in-law and on my dismissal.

For a time Somerville free lanced in London and then received an offer of an editorial chair on the *Catholic Register,* now the *Canadian Register.* This he accepted and for years was a prominent figure in the Catholic life of Toronto, being honoured, as have few Canadians, with a papal knighthood. He was a Knight Commander of St. Gregory.

"I have always recognized that the *Star* paid me a high compliment in firing me," he reminisced some years later. "I hate catering to low appetites as much as I ever did, but I have recognized since coming back to Canada, as I did not realize in London, the strength of the temptation to do what competitors are doing, and what seems necessary for success. . . . In England the population is large enough to allow different newspapers to specialize on catering for different tastes. We have the *Times* and the Daily *Express* in London, but in Toronto every paper must appeal to the mob."

# 33 ⋘

## Preacher in Print

THROUGH MY YEARS as editor of the *Weekly*, the *Star* offered a pulpit in print to many a preacher, but one of our most popular features in the twenties was the question and answer column conducted by the Rev. William A. Cameron.

In fact it became so popular that the burden of answering reader correspondence was too heavy and we had to discontinue it.

"Bill" Cameron, as he is known to most Torontonians and to the tens of thousands who have been among his radio audiences, was a country lad from Palmyra, Ontario. We had been together at Woodstock College and, at my wedding in 1908, he was my best man.

One of my prize possessions is a photo taken at Woodstock. It shows him fresh from the farm—a thin, rather ascetic face, a high pompadour of straw coloured hair, and a stiff white collar holding his head erect. Dressed in his Sunday best, he looked the personification of the typical young country parson.

Yet there are many advantages to being born in the country. He knew nothing of the five day, forty hour week. In his preaching, his pastoral visiting, his writing, and even in his badminton and golf, he was always a great worker.

At college Cameron was a good though not an outstanding student. But on the week-ends, in the pulpit of some little rural church, he would give his hearers everything he had in evangelical zeal and oratorical fire. Country congregations loved him. Cameron was a born revivalist, and his unusual gifts attracted the attention of prominent American laymen seeking a successor to the late Rev. Dr. R. A. Torrey who, with his singing partner Charles Alexander, had stirred the religious world to its depths in the first decade of this century. The young Canadian Baptist preacher was invited to travel the world round spreading the gospel fire at virtually his own salary.

But Cameron's answer was "No." He felt that if he gave his life to a church pastorate, he could not only lead men to Christ but aid them in their subsequent religious growth.

Even before his graduation in theology from McMaster University he was invited to become the minister of Toronto's Bloor Street Baptist Church, then housed in a small building at Bay (then North) and Bloor Streets. He rapidly became one of the city's most popular preachers. He was forced regularly to conduct two evening services prior to the First World War and, when he came back from his chaplaincy overseas, his deacons rented the 3,000 seat Uptown Theatre to accommodate the crowds. Even this giant auditorium was insufficient.

At this time radio arrived and Cameron was invited by the *Star's* pioneer station CFCA to become Canada's first radio preacher. For almost ten years he was on the air each Sunday, drawing mail which at times assumed mountainous proportions. The combination of his *Weekly* column and his Sunday airborne sermon made him Canada's best known pastor.

But he longed for a church home. The theatre accommodated great crowds but it was most difficult to create an atmosphere of worship. One day his church was offered $250,000 for its Bloor and Bay site. Another $300,000 cash was raised and with an initial debt of less than $100,000—long since paid—the beautiful stone Yorkminster Baptist Church, seating about 2,000 persons, was erected in north central Toronto.

My wife and I had joined Cameron's congregation in 1915 and, as a member of the building committee, I had suggested the name Yorkminster, a choice which was blessed when the Dean of York Minster sent a stone from a clerestory window of his ancient English cathedral to be built into the tower of Toronto's new Baptist church. For eighteen years I edited the church calendar, and was regularly elected to the Board of Deacons. Yorkminster was our church home.

One thing which contributed much to W. A. Cameron's success was his keen sense of humour. He had a great fund of stories which he could tell well, and was in demand as an after dinner speaker.

I recall a practical joke he played on a fellow ministerial student while at Woodstock College. A scarlet fever epidemic threatened. Word went round that the ban on smoking had been lifted since tobacco was supposed to kill germs. All over the residence boys produced forbidden cigars, cigarettes and pipes.

In one room a group of theologs were sampling the cure. W. E. Matthews, later minister in Winnipeg and Windsor, hesitantly accepted a pipe from Cameron, which the latter had mischievously filled with chewing tobacco. Three puffs and Matthews, deathly sick, headed for the window.

Bill Cameron married thousands of couples during his forty years, but one wedding early in his career, that of an old sea captain, all but cost him a good friend. When he pronounced the captain and his sweetheart man and wife, the groom, ill at ease, stood awkwardly still.

"Aren't you going to salute your bride?" asked the parson.

The old salt drew himself to attention, clicked his heels smartly together and, putting his hand to his forehead, "saluted" the bride in the approved naval fashion.

Cameron burst into a roar of laughter. The ancient mariner, angry and flushed, grabbed his newly acquired wife by the arm, and stamped out of the room. It took a lot of explaining to heal the wound.

It was not only in the size of his congregations and in his radio preaching and newspaper columnizing that Cameron established a unique ministry. Each Monday evening to his "confessional," people of all ages and faiths brought their problems, religious and personal. Wednesday meetings for prayer, bible study, and song were regularly held. Often he conducted four or five funerals in a day and as many weddings. Those released from prison received from him an early helping hand.

He authored a lengthy shelf of books, most of them containing sermons but one, *The Clinic of a Cleric,* tells of his experiences in meeting troubled souls and talking through their problems.

And he served the one congregation for four decades, from his call in 1908 until his retirement in the late forties. Indeed it was only after he left the Yorkminster pulpit, and its demanding round of duties and responsibilities, that Bill Cameron married and began to enjoy some of the rest and pleasure which he had commended to his parishioners over the years.

But even then he was not able to erase completely the printer's ink which had marked his fingers in those years with the *Star Weekly.* Today he is back in the pulpit of print, contributing a regular religious column to the editorial page of the *Daily Star,* as he did three decades ago for the *Weekly.*

# 34 ⫷⫷⫷

## The Colonel and the Character

WHEN I GRADUATED from McMaster University back in 1905 I stood
for a moment at the parting of the ways.

Colonel John Bayne Maclean, president of the Maclean Publishing
Company, invited me to join his staff and promised an early editorship
of one of his numerous trade journals. He pointed out, in addition
to the possibilities for advancement in his own organization, that
many of his editors had found positions of high responsibility in the
commercial and industrial world.

But I was not interested in a business career. I preferred the
many-sided contact with life offered by newspaper journalism, and
chose the *Star.*

My friendship with Col. Maclean, however, continued through
the years though he did not like my boss, J. E. Atkinson, and did not
hesitate to say so. The Colonel was an imperialist, a traditional
capitalist, and a conservative in outlook though tied to no party. He
had no confidence in the sincerity of the *Star's* president, and openly
referred to him as an opportunist who flirted with socialism and communism, not because he really believed in them, but because it was
profitable. Atkinson on the other hand termed the Colonel a survivor
of the outmoded dictatorial school of capitalism. Their mutual
antipathy was of long standing.

The Colonel loved to talk to me of his boyhood days. Both of
us were born in the same part of Ontario. His father was Rev.
Andrew Maclean, pioneer minister of the Presbyterian kirk at Crieff,
Puslinch Township, a few miles north-east of my native Galt.

Some years before his death, Colonel Maclean persuaded the

elders and congregation of the Crieff church to allow him to restore the manse in which he was born and to beautify the church and grounds. With his brother Hugh, he arranged an endowment to provide for their perpetual care.

Among the pioneer furniture which was put in the house were the horsehair sofa and chairs which had belonged to Dr. John Bayne, minister of my own Knox Church of Galt, after whom the Colonel was named. I remember my father telling of Dr. Bayne's sermons. Sunday School began at 9.30 a.m. and the congregation sat down to church an hour later. Preliminaries over, Dr. Bayne would preach until the adjournment for lunch and, at two o'clock, the members would reassemble for the conclusion of the sermon.

Colonel Maclean has, of course, other much more impressive monuments—the giant Maclean-Hunter publishing and printing plant on Yonge Street just north of Toronto and the large office building on the city's University Avenue. *Maclean's Magazine, Chatelaine, Mayfair,* the *Financial Post* and a host of trade journals bear perpetual testimony to his genius. Yet I cannot help but feel that his memories sleep most soundly in that precious bit of clapboard Canadiana which now will be preserved forever near Puslinch Lake.

*     *     *     *     *

Nor can I think back those many years without remembering Bernard Keble Sandwell.

He was my managing editor the three summer months of 1901 when I worked on the ill-fated Hamilton *Morning Post,* but between 1925 and 1932 we changed places and he contributed many delightful and satirical skits to the paper which I was editing.

In Hamilton "B. K." was the Poo Bah of the *Post.* He wrote the editorials, edited and wrote the headings for the city, telegraph, and sporting news, assigned reporters their jobs, and even supervised the woman's page. And all the experience he had to qualify him for his multiple editorial responsibilities were a B.A. degree; two years' secretarial work on a London, England, daily; and a few months as a cub reporter on England's *Hastings Observer.* He also had a fine intellectual appearance.

When the *Post* gave up its ghost, "B. K.'s" salary was over $400 in arrears. He was in a dentist's chair having four of his front teeth pulled when the bailiffs walked into the *Post* offices and took possession. "It was four years before I could afford a permanent denture," he laments.

When I asked him about it half a century later, Sandwell confessed that he had forgotten just how much the *Post* owed him. "But I know there were a lot of cheques I never cashed. I was using them for bookmarks."

"It is easy to see that he was not married then," interjected his wife who was listening in on our conversation.

Collapse of the *Post* left him stranded financially. He applied to J. E. Atkinson for a job. The *Star* president, while he had none available, offered Sandwell a railway pass to Montreal and a letter of introduction to the Montreal *Herald*. There he landed, at $10 a week, a position which called for him to cover everything from the latest developments in the morgue to the newest offerings in the theatre. Soon, however, after a stint as the *Herald's* city editor, he was promoted to the editorial page.

In 1911 Sandwell accepted first the assistant editorship and later the post of chief editor of Montreal's *Financial Times*. Eight years later "B. K." became assistant to Stephen Leacock as professor of economics at McGill University, and in 1923 went to Queen's as professor of English and head of that department.

After two brief years at Queen's University, and just as he was stepping on board ship with his wife for a summer in England, Sandwell received word that he had been fired. But time heals all wounds. Seventeen years later the same university conferred on him an honorary Doctorate of Laws, and the students elected him Rector in succession to the Earl of Athlone.

From 1925 to 1932 Sandwell made his living as a free lance writer in Montreal. It was then that he appeared on the pages of the *Star Weekly* as well as contributing regularly to *Saturday Night*. When the latter's editor, Hector Charlesworth, resigned in 1932 to become chairman of the Canadian Broadcasting Commission, Sandwell succeeded to his post which he held with great distinction until his retirement in June, 1951.

Anyone who entered the *Saturday Night* building expecting to see the man whose photo appeared regularly with his special articles was sure to be disappointed. The photo was undoubtedly a fair representation of editor Sandwell when he was dressed up, his hair parted and brushed smooth. But it was not like him when he was at work. In the old days at Hamilton his great shock of wavy hair was never tidy, and the habit persisted. Some editors may be able to think without mussing their hair, but not Sandwell.

Like many other newspaper men, possibly most of them, "B. K." had an untidy office. His desk was piled high with newspapers and clippings. There were shelves of reference books, and a typewriter desk where he did his writing. His working suit, wrote Thelma LeCoq, looked "as though he had bought it off one rack and hung it on another," while his hat had "those bends which are referred to as having character."

*Saturday Night,* in the days of Sandwell, was not a paper for the masses. It was, if anything, a bit highbrow, and offered a market for people who thought they had something important to say and usually had. There was no comic section—heaven forbid!—and few cartoons, but generally there were a number of bright and breezy articles to liven up its pages. Sandwell latterly confined his activities to his "Front Page," to editorials, to his delightfully witty "Passing Show" column of brief paragraphs, and a special article, which as often as not, was on art or the theatre. He has a marvellous gift of being able to get to the root of almost any question in a few words, and then, by a probing sentence, to expose the weakness of the thing he is attacking.

To quote Miss LeCoq again:

The only regular habit he has is that of being constantly irregular. He has no set hours for coming to work, no set time for doing anything. He is apt to leave town for a few days without mentioning it to anyone.

It is as an after dinner speaker that "B. K." really shines, and he has a theory that the way to please people is to insult them in a good humoured way. Once he introduced a Toronto audience to a visiting lecturer by saying: "You see before you a fairly complete cross section of the intelligentsia of this city. I hope you are not too depressed."

Speaking to the Canadian Authors' Association, he termed it "a group where virgins of sixty write poems of passion."

Sandwell has always had a keen interest in things dramatic. This may have dated from the time when, as a student, he appeared on the professional stage with the "divine Sarah Bernhardt." Pin him down to it, however, and he will admit that he was one of a crowd of supers hired at the university to rush on stage and shout "en bas le courtisane!"

But nothing gives him more pleasure than the theatre. He says he would like to have been a dramatist or a novelist, but is quite sure he could never create a character.

Anyone who has met this man with his shock of white hair, his dominating nose and ears, and his Churchillian pink complexion may be forgiven for differing.

B. K. Sandwell has no need to create a character.

He is one.

# 35 ⋘

## *Weekly Stars*

As EDITOR OF THE *Star Weekly* in its early days, I found my small budget both a handicap and a blessing. Since we could not often afford to buy big names, we had a double reason for opening our columns to newcomers. And, in so doing, we gave a start to men and women who today are writers of wide renown.

The very first article I bought from Mary Lowry (now Mary Lowry Ross) was a piece about the midway at the Toronto Exhibition. It sparkled with wit and liveliness. The second was just as good, only more difficult to read. Her typewriter ribbon was apparently both faint from old age, and full of holes. Would she *please,* I asked, get a new one. But she was canny, then as now. She could read her work; why couldn't I? Besides, how did she know I would buy any more articles? The next article was still less legible. As politely as I knew how, I pleaded with her to get a new ribbon. Finally she did.

After she had written a number of articles for the *Weekly,* she became a member of the *Daily* staff. She was sent to cover the convention of the Pan-American League of Women Voters at Baltimore, attended by such notables as Emmeline Pankhurst and Carrie Chapman Catt. A heated row developed behind the scenes, from which the press was excluded. But all the newspapers except the *Star* carried columns about the exciting rumpus. Unschooled in newspaper ways, and out of shame and loyalty to her sex, Mary suppressed the whole story.

But before she left to become B. K. Sandwell's ace of trumps on *Saturday Night,* she had developed a real nose for headline news.

\* \* \* \* \*

Morley Callaghan says, that when I bought his first article for the *Star Weekly,* he was but eighteen, and in the fifth form at high school. It was about a street meeting at the corner of Yonge and Albert Streets. "To my surprise, you printed it," he says. The date was August 6, 1921.

Morley had a part time job for one summer on the *Daily Star*, came back the following summer on full time, then worked at "space rates" for the winter. On graduation from university, he joined the staff. But he was never very keen on newspaper work. "I was fired about five times," he says, "but it never became official, and I parted amiably enough with Hindmarsh. He told me I presented the whole problem of the university man. I had never been broken to harness."

*   *   *   *   *

In her fascinating story, *Confessions of an Immigrant's Daughter*, Laura Goodman Salverson tells how she got her start as a writer:

When every other periodical rejected with cryptic dismissal my human interest tales of the pioneers, Mr. Cranston found them sufficiently meritorious to publish. These short stories supported my books. Their earnings paid for the preparation of manuscripts. These *Star* stories also made it possible for me to undertake the research required for historical novels.

Mrs. Salverson's sketches were so good that I could not refuse them. I am happy that I was able to give her a helping hand while she was writing her now famous Icelandic-Canadian novels.

*   *   *   *   *

When Claire Wallace applied to Hindmarsh for a job on the *Star*, he told her he didn't like women reporters because they cried when things went wrong. The truth was that Claire's family—two of her brothers were on the *Star*—had begged him to turn her down.

But Claire refused to be ignored. Her father, long before, had published a weekly newspaper at Orangeville, and had become assistant city editor of the *Star* before joining the executive staff of the Confederation Life. Printers' ink was in her blood.

Finally she persuaded Hindmarsh to look at some of her work. He liked it, began taking her articles on a free lance basis, and then sent her along to me with the suggestion that she might write something for the *Weekly*.

Tall, blonde and good looking, Claire was extremely shy and nervous, a handicap she declares she has never wholly overcome, though few would now suspect it. Her radiant, happy personality has won her hosts of fans.

Unlike so many aspiring writers, she brought her own ideas with her. She rang doorbells to find out about the work and wages of Toronto's domestic servants. She tried to get a taxi driver's licence and failed. She advertised that she was a widow with $25,000 to invest, got hundreds of letters and a good story. At last Hindmarsh took her on the *Daily* staff and, some years later, she went into radio. Today she stands in the front rank of Canadian broadcasters.

*       *       *       *       *

Arthur D. "Cowboy" Kean, who for some years thrilled the *Weekly's* readers with his western stories, never was a cowboy. He detested the name. He belonged to that aristocracy of horsemen who proudly claim to "make horses gentle for cowboys to ride."

Kean knew everything there was to know about horses. His whole life, prior to the time he struck Toronto in the middle twenties, had been spent on British Columbia horse farms—breeding, raising, breaking and training horses for sale to cattle ranchers throughout the Canadian West.

He brought with him a letter of introduction to J. E. Atkinson from Sir Edward Beatty, then president of the Canadian Pacific Railway. Beatty said that if Kean could write as well as he could talk, he would be a winner. Atkinson read Kean's first story, "Shorty, the Cupid Horse," liked it, and sent him down to me. From then on we published one of his animal yarns in every issue. The *Weekly* printed altogether some 250 of them.

Of medium height, thickset, and with slightly bowed legs, Kean brought with him the tang of the open air and was very popular around the *Star*. For some years he had a small farm in the Don Valley north of Toronto and there kept a few horses, demonstrating his prowess again and again. Owners brought their "unbreakable" horses to him and he rode them into submission, but never unkindly.

Kean came from the Okanagan Lake district of British Columbia where "Ogo Pogo," the legendary sea serpent, made periodic appearances. When I suggested that we might introduce "Ogo Pogo" to the crowds at the Canadian National Exhibition, he agreed enthusiastically. A sea serpent was manufactured from wood, painted canvas, and old tires, and equipped with a terrifying head. The theory was that it would travel submerged behind a motorboat, emerging only when the towing craft speeded up. Kean hired a boat and pulled the serpent out through the western gap and along the sea wall. It was towed by a rope several hundred feet long and travelled under water splendidly.

But when the throttle was opened up, the horrible beast, instead of stretching its ugly head out of the waters of Lake Ontario, merely toppled over, snapped the tow rope, and disintegrated in the heavy swells. It was one of the very few times Kean failed to make the headlines.

\*     \*     \*     \*     \*

One of the most colourful of the *Star Weekly's* desk men was John Herries McCulloch, a dour Scot of sterling character and unquestioned loyalty. He was born in the ancient kingdom of Galloway in southwestern Scotland and, like so many others from the land of the heather, came to Canada in search of wider opportunities. He brought with him a marked Scottish accent, a pawky wit that did not shrink from a laugh at his own expense, and a fine English style, at times almost poetic.

After several years on a western farm, he enrolled at the Ontario Agricultural College. On graduation, equipped with a degree in Scientific Agriculture, he entered farm journalism. But Mac's Galloway origin, and his love for historical research and romance, soon led to a study of the thrilling story of the Selkirk Settlers. From his pen came *The Men of Kildonan,* a novel of the trying journey from the Strath of Kildonan in Sutherlandshire to the banks of Manitoba's Red River. It was an outstanding contribution to Canadiana, and I bought the rights to reproduce it in the *Star Weekly.* Subsequently McCulloch submitted a number of articles on other topics, and still later accepted an invitation to join my staff.

After twenty-four years in Canada, Mac went back home. He had found both the personnel and editorial policies of the *Star* repugnant to his Scottish code. Today, he lives with his Canadian wife in Edinburgh's Frederick Street where, from the windows of his century-old third storey flat, one has a magnificent view of the Castle. He has done extremely well for himself. Special staff writer for Lord Beaverbrook's *Scottish Express,* he has also authored a number of books, many of them historical, and his *Scottish Sheep Dogs and Their Masters* has become a classic.

McCulloch loves a joke on himself and on his fellow Scots. He told me, when we were last together in his Edinburgh home, of an aristocrat named Jamieson who made the fatal mistake of marrying a McCulloch. Not only did his wife make life intolerable for him on earth but, when he finally died and went to hell, he found the place terribly inhospitable and cold.

"There were too many McCullochs standing around the fire," explained Mac with a chuckle.

\* \* \* \* \*

Merrill Denison, whose pen is now as well known in the United States as in Canada, was a regular contributor to the *Star Weekly,* and his fine sense of humour had full play in the stunt stories on which he worked with Gregory Clark. Stephen Leacock did for us a series of articles which we shared with the Montreal *Star.* If ever a man looked less like a university professor and more like the traditional stage farmer, it was he. Leacock cared not an iota for his appearance. His clothes fitted him like a sack, and his hair was always in a hopeless tangle. It was not always easy to understand what he was saying either but, when one did, it was generally fun.

\* \* \* \* \*

Toronto Public School Inspector James L. Hughes wrote frequently for us. His most notable contribution was his autobiography, chuck full of the good humoured egotism characteristic of both Hughes brothers, Sir Sam and James L.

J. L. Hughes was intensely British and he told how, when crossing into the United States south of Winnipeg, he was asked the customary string of questions by the American immigration officer.

To the query: "Are you an American citizen?" J. L. replied: "No, thank God!"

The officer blinked but went on. "Is it your intention to take up residence in the United States?"

"No, sir!" said Hughes firmly.

"Thank God!" ejaculated the U.S. officer.

\* \* \* \* \*

One of the *Star Weekly* authors with whom I have maintained close contact through the years is Louis Arthur Cunningham, writer of Canadian historical romances. He is a Maritimer and proud of it. He gets a lot of fun out of life, and seldom stirs from his country home near New Brunswick's Hammond River. He never could see "the sense of going away from home in a car or a train only to turn around and come back where I started from."

Despite the fact that Cunningham believes firmly in the study of the classical languages as an essential foundation for a good English style, his literary *modus operandi* is based on somewhat less rigid rules.

"Sometimes I do not write anything for weeks on end," he confessed to me one day. "The idea of a daily writing stint is all wrong. I write when I feel like it, or when I realize I will be hungry if I don't. There is no incentive like hunger to get a fellow going. Writing is just like any other work. You just do it. If a chap waited until he got inspiration, I am afraid there would not be much done. When I have a good day I write as many as 8,000 to 10,000 words. I cannot type. I write everything in long hand and my wife types it into saleable shape. She is a mighty clever woman. She can read whole sentences of my writing when I have not the slightest idea what they are all about."

Now, all over this continent and the British Isles, thousands of people read Cunningham's sentences and, if they don't have the slightest idea what they are all about, at least they keep coming back for more.

\* \* \* \* \*

Not the least interesting of our *Star Weekly* contributors was Hugh Templin, editor and publisher of the *News-Record* of Fergus, a central Ontario town built of stone and Scots.

Looking over the Fergus weekly one day I came across a humorous skit which Hugh had written. I asked if he would be interested in submitting a somewhat longer yarn in similar style for use in the *Star Weekly*. Thus was born a series of amusing village tales published over the pen name of "Ephraim Acres."

Not only through his unique editorial page, which he composes at the linotype keyboard, has Templin served his community. From his pen and presses have come an excellent local history, *Fergus, The Story of a Little Town*. His campaigning through the years led to the erection of the Shand storage dam on the Grand River near Fergus, a project which has already saved scores of thousands of dollars annually in flood losses. Hugh Templin is more than a newspaper editor. He has been a consecrated community servant, a fact which the University of Western Ontario recognized when it recently conferred on him an honorary doctorate of laws.

I put Hugh Templin LL.D. last in this chapter because through him, and his Ephraim Acres, I recalled and recaptured the love of smaller places—and of smaller papers—which was soon to guide me away from the spinning rotary presses of metropolitan journalism to quieter and greener hills.

# 36 ⫷

## *The Man Who Stayed to Dinner*

MEMBERS OF THE *Star* staff used to wonder what would happen when the Chief was gone. Would control pass to his son, Joseph Junior, or to his son-in-law, H. C. Hindmarsh?

The contrast in the personalities of the two men was striking. Joseph Atkinson, Junior, was a comparative newcomer at the *Star* when I was there. He was a slightly-built young man, shy and retiring, with a pleasant, friendly disposition which made him popular everywhere. He had never been reporter or editor, nor had he been closely associated with the business office. He seemed to have many of his father's good qualities, but he was entirely unassertive.

Harry Hindmarsh was big, confident and aggressive, and a thorough newspaperman. Under his editorial management the *Star's* circulation had climbed steadily, and he had given evidence of great business ability. He had married the Chief's only daughter, Ruth, and was one of the family.

J. E. Atkinson's answer was to bequeath the paper to the Atkinson Charitable Foundation. He named a board of directors to carry on the Foundation and the paper, of which Joseph Junior and Hindmarsh are both members. The board elected Joseph Junior as chairman and Hindmarsh as president. Mrs. Hindmarsh has since been appointed to a vacancy on the board, so that the Hindmarshes have two votes to the younger Atkinson's one. Indeed the Chairman of the Board has recently confessed that very often he is a minority of one in the Foundation's decisions.

Joseph Atkinson Junior inherited his father's flair for machinery. He soon made himself the master of every mechanical detail in the big newspaper plant. His special interest was the fleet of *Star* motor vehicles, whose activities he supervised, and his hobby today, modestly indulged, is collecting and operating for his own pleasure early model automobiles.

Hindmarsh, on the other hand, had come up through the editorial department, and had worked in close association with Atkinson Senior in developing the policies which had won such glittering success for the *Star*. They made a strong team. Atkinson, with his keen business sense, watched every penny of expenditure. Hindmarsh, bent on scoring triumphs of sensational news coverage, tended to spend money lavishly. Atkinson was proud of his son-in-law's spectacular exploits as an editor, but kept a firm hand on the purse strings. If Hindmarsh exceeded his budget one month, he had to scrimp the next. On more than one occasion, while I sat in his office, he was the recipient of a telephonic rap over the knuckles from the Chief. He would accept the reprimand humbly, and when it was over smile uncomfortably and comment, "Well, that's that for today."

"H. C. H.," as he is known to most journalists, had joined the *Daily Star* staff in November, 1911. After a year on the city hall beat, he was made assistant city editor, then wire editor, and, when C. C. Campbell was retired, he became city editor. In 1916 he combined this job with that of assistant managing editor, and, when John R. Bone died in 1928, he stepped into the managing editor's post.

Because of his massive frame—he was over six feet three inches and weighed 225 pounds—his squarish head with close-cropped hair, heavy-lidded eyes, ponderous walk and dominating disposition, the legend ran that he was of Prussian descent. But the facts do not support this theory. His mother was Etoile Comfort, daughter of Hiram Comfort, a wealthy woollen manufacturer of St. Thomas, Ontario. His father, Harry Frank Hindmarsh, was a painter and decorator in St. Thomas, and a horn player in the citizens' band. He and his wife moved to Bismarck, Missouri, where he became a railway telegrapher and here the son was born. Following her husband's death, Mrs. Hindmarsh returned to St. Thomas. Having inherited her father's estate, she was able to give her son the best of everything.

Boyhood acquaintances say that Harry was a shy lad who did not readily mix. The same could be said of the mature Hindmarsh. He was fond of cats, dogs and music. He played the violin, cornet and bugle. His love of animals was later reflected in the pages of the *Star Weekly;* his musical bent in the *Star* radio hour of recorded music, the programmes for which he often selects himself.

His mother being a Baptist, Harry attended the Baptist Church and Sunday school. When he reached college age, however, the Baptist preacher, a man of strong prejudices, warned him against "that Godless institution, the University of Toronto." Hindmarsh promptly disregarded that advice by enrolling in University College; and, in my day, seemed to have a strong dislike for anything Baptist. The time came, however, when he applied to McMaster University for permission to enrol two of his sons.

At the University of Toronto, Hindmarsh showed his innate ability for newspaper work on the staff of *The Varsity*. Under his editorship it was changed from a weekly literary magazine to a semi-weekly newspaper. On graduation in 1909 he joined the reporting staff of the Toronto *Globe,* but night work as cable editor affected his eyesight and he resigned to become publicity man for a firm of Toronto brokers. He found this job unexciting, and left it to join the *Star*.

I can write of Harry Hindmarsh only as I knew him on the *Star* between 1911 and 1933. I am told that in later years he has mellowed greatly, and that his relations with his staff are on a pleasanter basis. It is said that economy waves and wholesale firings have ceased. The Toronto Newspaper Guild, crushed in Atkinson's day after a bitter struggle, has now been recognized. *Star* reporters, special writers, artists and others have a new sense of security. Salaries are the highest paid by any Canadian newspaper.

But in my day Hindmarsh was not regarded with affection. Nor did he want to be so regarded. He did not encourage informality or friendship. Seldom did he call anyone by his first name. It was always Mister So-and-So.

He was himself a hard worker, and regular in his habits. When he was city editor, he rose early in his Oakville home to catch a train that would enable him to be in his office by nine o'clock. With him he brought a list of assignments he had compiled from a study of the morning papers. Sometimes these placed an impossible burden on an individual, and had to be revised. Hard on himself, he expected the utmost in work and enterprise from his staff.

But men of ability and strong individuality found his rule tyrannical and his manner unbearable, and were often provoked to rebellion that ended in resignation or dismissal. It was his policy to deflate egos that seemed to him to be overblown. When a reporter covered an important assignment, his articles were given a by-line and he got due credit for outstanding work. But if he came home holding his head a little too high, he would be quickly brought low. Hindmarsh would assign him to a job normally given to a cub, to show him that it was the *Star's* glory and not his own that mattered. One of Hindmarsh's favourite remarks was: "We want no prima donnas around here."

Sometimes, when the "prima donna" revolted, there were exciting moments in the office. Former members of the staff recall the day when an angry reporter, now editor of one of Canada's leading dailies, hurled an inkwell at the managing editor's head, missed it, and turned the wall beyond into an inky mess. Or the day when another scribe, now a prominent Toronto business executive, warned Hindmarsh that if he came a step nearer he would turn him upside down and stick him in the wastepaper basket. And the scribe was big enough to have made a good try.

Hindmarsh showed an amazing capacity for sensing the kind of story that has wide popular appeal, and when he got wind of such a story, he would go "all out" to get it, putting all the resources of his staff to work, and sparing no expense. He would send reporters around the world on a foraging expedition, leaving it to them to dig up interesting material. *Star* men learned that the only unpardonable sin was failure to come through with a good story; no one was ever fired for spending too much money if he turned in something Hindmarsh liked.

I can remember only one instance when Hindmarsh's instinct for spotting a big story failed him. When the Dionne quintuplets were born, a reporter on the North Bay *Nugget* wired the *Star* offering details. Hindmarsh instructed Wire Editor Gerald Brown to ask for a hundred words. Thus the *Star* muffed what turned out to be one of the biggest "human interest" stories of the decade. Next day, however, the error was rectified, and for months the *Star* featured the Quints in a lavish manner.

Those who disliked Hindmarsh used to say that he had done his best to live down his middle name, Comfort. Certainly no other newspaper man in Canada can have made more people uncomfortable. That applies not only to men and women who have been hired and fired by him, but to thousands who have been under the *Star's* news spotlight. On the other hand, his admirers (and there are many who are still *Star* employees) declare that the name rightly belongs to him, and point to examples of Hindmarsh's kindness and consideration that have brought comfort to them and their families.

Big physically, he loved big things and he liked to do things in a big way. On his desk in my day was a giant fountain pen at least a foot long, with a barrel nearly an inch in diameter, a gift from his mother when he became city editor. He drove a large car, and had Great Danes as pets. He dressed quietly, favouring grey clothes and wearing rimless glasses. When pleased, he was capable of a friendly smile, but he seldom laughed. When angry, he flushed a deep red.

He was proud of the *Star's* editorial independence. A former *Star* man once told me of reporting to Hindmarsh after being sent to interview a man who had a story that seemed to warrant publicity. "I told him the *Star* would co-operate," said the reporter. Hindmarsh bridled. "That is a word that should never be used in connection with the *Star*," he exclaimed.

When expenses had to be cut, or he suspected hostility to his orders, he was capable of dealing ruthlessly with individuals.

Once, during the depression of the '30's, he ordered the discharge of my make-up man. I sent him a note explaining that the man, who himself suffered from eye-trouble, had recently been put to the expense of an operation on the eyes of his baby, and urged that he be kept on the staff for the time being. His reply noted that the man's mother, who ran a grocery store, would be able to take care of him and his family. I pointed out that the business was a small one, and could hardly stand that strain. Back came the terse note: "As Mr. —— and his family will not be reduced to actual privation, the order will stand." Members of the *Star Weekly* staff made up a purse of over $100 for the discharged man, and I arranged with the eye specialist to cut down his fee for the operation. Shortly after, the victim of this economy wave managed to get a job on another city paper.

When nearly all my staff artists were drafted for a whole week to do retouching work for a jewellery catalogue that was being printed on the rotogravure press, I had to hire outside artists in order to get out the paper.

When I told Hindmarsh what I had been forced to do, he was furious. My own artists, he declared, should have done the work in overtime. I told him that one of them, "Deacon" Johnston, had worked for sixteen hours one day on the catalogue. Hindmarsh told me to fire him. I inquired why.

"Hasn't he been complaining?" he fumed. "No," I said. "If anyone is complaining, I am the one."

"Fire him anyway," said Hindmarsh. I told him that since the fault, if any, was mine, it would mean firing me too. Hindmarsh calmed down, and neither of us was fired.

Yet Harry Hindmarsh was often considerate and kind to individuals on his staff. He does not drink, and regards those who do as weaklings, yet he has shown great patience with reporters who had become alcoholics. They have been given treatment at the *Star's* expense and their families looked after in the meantime.

If a reporter got into financial troubles and appealed to Hindmarsh, he would listen sympathetically, ask for details of all debts, write a cheque for the total and then supervise the man's pay envelopes, often with the aid of the wife, until everything was paid off.

It is said that J. E. Atkinson, unimpressed by the kind of young men who were calling on his daughter, Ruth, brought Harry Hindmarsh home one night to dinner. The courtship that ensued ended in Hindmarsh becoming the Chief's son-in-law. There is another story to the effect that after the wedding Atkinson told Hindmarsh he should find another job; he did not want a son-in-law on the paper. But Hindmarsh had given such proofs of his capacity that he had little difficulty in breaking down this objection.

In any calling, marriage to the boss's daughter usually helps. But no one who knows Hindmarsh could doubt that he would have climbed as high, if not so fast, without this aid.

# 37 «««

## *Selling Papers to Little People*

IT WAS THE AIM of J. E. Atkinson to produce a newspaper that would
have big circulation, big advertising, and big profits.

With the aid of two great managing editors, Bone and Hindmarsh,
he evolved a formula so effective that it won for the *Star* a circulation
far exceeding that of any other Canadian daily, and made its publisher
a multi-millionaire.

He did not aim at making the *Daily Star* a great newspaper in the
sense that the London *Times,* the New York *Times,* the Manchester
*Guardian* and the *Christian Science Monitor* are great. These papers
seek to present and interpret important news as fully and impartially
as possible. They are not concerned with building up huge circula-
tions, and do not exist solely to make money.

Atkinson shrewdly perceived that what the average Canadian
wanted in his newspaper was not instruction on the more serious
aspects of the news, but entertainment and amusement. And since his
objective was a big circulation, he must meet the tastes and preferences
of this wider public. He must win favour in every section of the
community large enough to provide a sizable body of readers.

This policy has been well expressed by B. K. Sandwell who wrote
of Atkinson:

He early saw that power was beginning to shift from the rich and
important to the little people in the semi-detached houses, and he
began to address himself to these alone. Circulation is the essence of
publishing, and circulation was all that he cared for. He went out to
get it in every direction, conscious that once he had the biggest
circulation in Toronto, no advertiser could afford to stay out of his
paper, no matter how much he disliked it.

Thus it became the policy of the *Star* to give the lion's share of its space to those things in which the ordinary reader found most interest—the colourful and "human interest" aspects of the news—at the expense of matters of more serious import. Accidents, disasters, crimes, dramatic or picturesque happenings of all kinds, received its major attention, filling columns with words, pictures and headlines. Controversies were sired to stir up excitement and promote sales. Many an innocent remark made in public speech or interview was blown up into a provocative challenge. Men were spurred into statements which would make *Star* headlines. The *Star* maintained a large reporting staff, and a corps of reporters was turned loose on any event that had sensational possibilities. No expense was spared in sending men on long journeys to get a colourful story.

Some of the *Star's* exploits have become classics of newspaper enterprise. One resulted in the greatest "scoop" in North American newspaper annals. When in April, 1928, the German airship, Bremen, crash-landed in Labrador after making the first east-west Atlantic crossing, Hindmarsh, who had just become managing editor, commissioned Duke Schiller, noted bush pilot, to fly to the scene, get story and pictures, and return to Lake Agnes. The cost was $7,000. A special train was engaged to rush Fred Griffin, Roy Greenaway and Ralph Whitman to Lake Agnes. The *Star* men fought off six American newsmen who tried to climb aboard. At Murray Bay, Griffin gave the telegraph operator a copy of the *New Republic* and ordered him to telegraph it to the *Star,* word for word, thus keeping all competing reporters off the wire. When Schiller flew in with his precious file, an American reporter grabbed it, but Griffin grappled with him and regained possession. Then he put it on a *Star* plane. When the plane was forced down in Quebec, a train was hired to take it to Montreal, whence it was rushed to Toronto by taxi. The *Star* had a twenty-four hour world-beat on the news.

When the late King George VI and Queen Elizabeth came to Canada, Hindmarsh detailed seventy reporters to cover their tour. Their Majesties were never out of sight of a *Star* man except when they retired for the night. When they arrived in Toronto, the *Star* building was the most lavishly decorated of any in the city. Over the doorway was a life-size photo of the King and Queen and the two princesses walking in the grounds of Windsor Castle. Claude Pascoe of the *Star* staff discovered that the chauffeur of the royal car was an old wartime pal who had served with him in the Black Watch. The rest was easy. When Their Majesties were passing the *Star* building the chauffeur pointed to the huge photo and cried, "Look, Your Majesties!" Being human, the royal couple looked up at their likenesses and smiled. Fifteen *Star* photographers at various points of vantage snapped. Next day the best of these photos was printed in six columns on the *Star's* front page.

In July, 1926, fifteen young men were drowned when their canoe capsized in Balsam Lake. Hindmarsh ordered fifteen of his reporters to climb into a canoe, paddle out into Lake Ontario, and capsize the canoe, while cameramen recorded the scene reconstructing the tragedy.

The *Star* maintained Matthew Halton in England as resident correspondent to report on interesting aspects of British life, visit European capitals, and cover international gatherings and conferences. It employed Pierre van Paassen to visit Germany in 1933 and write articles on the rise of the Nazis, as a result of which the *Star* was banned by Hitler. Halton also went to Germany on a similar quest. It sent Gordon Sinclair around the world four times to write impressions of remote countries. Gregory Clark covered the coronation of King George VI, and he and Frederick Griffin made special trips to Britain on other occasions. During the Second World War, Gregory Clark's story of the British escape from Dunkirk, and Fred Griffin's tales of the D-Day invasion of France, were notable examples of war-reporting.

The *Star* has made a specialty of new medical discoveries. It was the first to give the world the story of the Banting-Best discovery of insulin. Reporters are sent far and wide to investigate miracle cures.

The *Star* was the first Canadian newspaper to recognize the value of pictures. In the early days, staff artists made black and white drawings of news events and personalities. Later the *Star* cameramen took their place, and news photos occupied an increasing share of space. The *Star* was also the first Canadian paper to use airplanes to cover news events, and the first to fly pictures across the ocean.

Feature material of various kinds combines with colourful treatment of the news to provide its readers with entertainment. The *Star* syndicate department secures the Canadian rights to a wide range of comic strips and other features, uses the best, and disposes of the balance to non-competing newspapers. Thus features which it does not wish to use itself can be kept away from its competitors.

Every type of promotion scheme has been tried by the *Star* in its bid for circulation—guessing games, quizzes, puzzles, beautiful child contests, animal-naming competitions, and so on *ad infinitum*. Serialization of books with a wide popular appeal, accompanied by much preliminary fanfare and attendant publicity, was for a time one of its most successful methods of gaining new readers.

By giving extensive and sympathetic publicity to the labour side in industrial disputes and to all matters affecting the interests of the working classes, Atkinson encouraged *Star* readers to regard the paper as the champion of the poor against the rich. Trade union affairs, strikes, workers' organizations of all kinds, were reported in a manner that indicated a friendly attitude towards labour. I recall running a series of articles in the *Star Weekly*, at Atkinson's suggestion, dealing with Canadian profit-sharing experiments. I thought at the time that he was interested in gathering information which would be helpful in devising a profit-sharing plan for the *Star*. But no such plan was ever initiated.

Between the wars, because of the space devoted to Russia, the *Star* was accused of Communist leanings. It sent Frederick Griffin and other writers to the Soviet Union, and they wrote glowing reports of what they saw there. The movement by communists to mobilize a "popular front" against war and fascism, and organizations to foster Canadian-Soviet friendship, were given extensive publicity. But the ruthlessness of Stalin's regime, and the activities of the Comintern, fostered a growing hostility to the Soviet Union and its domestic and foreign policies. The *Star* was blamed for misleading Canadians, and was referred to by its critics as the Toronto *Daily Pravda*.

Favourable publicity given by the *Star* to the newly organized CCF, a democratic Socialist party, only served to increase the dislike of those who saw in the *Star* a dangerous enemy of the capitalist system in Canada. When the *Star*, dropping its socialist pretensions, continued to throw the full weight of its support behind the Liberal Party at election time, its critics called Atkinson a hypocrite and opportunist.

The attention given to Russia so angered its Catholic readers that on January 3, 1939, Father Lanphier of the Radio League of St. Michael's Cathedral, addressed Atkinson on the air, and threatened to "go to the ecclesiastical authorities of the province, and ask them to ban your paper from our homes should the *Star* persist in glorification of Russian and Red doctrines." *Star* executives went into a huddle, and next day Gregory Clark set out for Rome to cover the election and installation of the Pope. A *Star* artist did a rush job on a portrait of the new Pontiff, while the rotogravure presses were kept waiting.

The aggressiveness of *Star* reporters in quest of anything that might prove sensational or stir up controversy often led to attempts to invade legitimate privacy. One day two *Star* reporters, Roy Greenaway and Bill Wiggins, were sent to cover a meeting in Massey Hall at which street railway employees were to discuss possible strike action. The meeting was a closed one, but the reporters were instructed to get into the hall by hook or crook, hide themselves, and listen to what was said. They managed to gain entry, and crouched behind the big organ pipes at the back of the stage. There they were discovered by a tiler, and roughly handled. Greenaway got a bloody nose, and Wiggins cuts over the eye and on the back of the head. Both required treatment at St. Michael's Hospital.

Atkinson defended all these practices on the score that he was specializing on news that was of current interest to the majority of readers, while giving a fair show to the interests of minorities. His critics maintained that he was simply seeking favour in any quarter that could supply more readers for the *Star*, without regard for the more serious consequences to the community, and for the established system of free enterprise under which the *Star* was flourishing. But while the *Star's* primary object was to provide exciting news and popular entertainment, and it would go to any length to secure these for its readers, Atkinson frequently made the *Star* the spearhead in a battle for some cause. On such occasions the full resources of the paper would be marshalled, and both news and editorial columns used to overwhelm opposition.

The *Star* was a big factor in bringing about the public ownership and development of hydro power in Ontario. It fought for the purchase of the Toronto Electric Light and Power Company by the city. Yet it waged an equally strenuous war against the grandiose scheme of Sir Adam Beck to cover Ontario with a network of electric railways.

During the reciprocity campaign of 1911, the *Star* employed ingenious methods in its effort to prove that Laurier's proposed pact with the United States would benefit Canadians. It sent reporters to Buffalo to buy pork, bologna and other meat products, and displayed these in the *Star's* windows, with price tags to show how much less was the retail price in the United States. Some Conservative business men cancelled their advertising with the paper that was featuring "Buffalo baloney." The campaign cost the *Star* many thousands of dollars, but established Atkinson's reputation for fearless and skilful fighting. The election over, the advertisers returned.

Men who incurred Atkinson's enmity felt the powerful sting of the *Star's* lash. When Premier Mitchell Hepburn of Ontario crossed swords with Mackenzie King, the Provincial Liberal chieftain was pursued relentlessly by the *Star* in a series of ruthless attacks. So vicious were the *Star's* assaults on George Drew, as Premier of Ontario and leader of the Progressive-Conservative party at Ottawa, that Drew launched and won a libel suit against the paper. A new trial was granted and settlement reached out of court.

The *Star* is not above using its headlines to give a slant to news stories or promote its policies, especially during election campaigns. But nothing of this kind has ever exceeded the eight-column heading in which it sought to discredit Drew, during the federal election of 1949, when he was leading the Progressive-Conservative forces and Camilien Houde, mayor of Montreal, was an independent candidate. The heading read:

KEEP CANADA BRITISH

DESTROY DREW'S HOUDE

GOD SAVE THE KING

Underneath a large picture of Houde, which emphasized his unattractive features, was the caption in large type: "By promise of a Drew and Duplessis contract Houde would sit in the federal cabinet as a contact man."

Premier Howard Ferguson of Ontario was another whom the *Star* fought with every weapon at its command. Stories of trouble between Ferguson and his ministers were part of the procedure. At last, on September 18, 1930, Ferguson had the following notice posted at Queen's Park:

> THE TORONTO STAR *is barred from all official sources of information and all offices of the Parliament Building, following the* STAR's *refusal to retract a story declaring that Dr. Forbes Godfrey, Minister of Health, had defied Premier Ferguson and refused to resign his portfolio, thus holding up reorganization of the cabinet.*

Ferguson said he had been told by the *Star's* legislature reporter that the story had been "written in the *Star* office," and that there would be no retraction.

The *Star* eventually had its privileges at the parliament buildings restored, but relations with the Ferguson government remained far from cordial.

It was Premier Ferguson who suggested that the *Star's* billboard slogan, "The Toronto Paper with the Largest Circulation," should be amended by adding the words "and the Smallest Influence."

But the fact was that the *Star* had become so strong that it could ignore both the jibes and the threats of its enemies, and its support or opposition had become a factor to be reckoned with in politics and in the conflict of social forces.

# 38 «««

## Publisher and Man

FEW NEWSPAPER PUBLISHERS have been the object of such warm regard and such bitter hatred as the late J. E. Atkinson.

When he died on May 8, 1949, the *Star* printed seventy-six columns about its president and his career in one issue. Subsequent issues carried still more.

Public men and women throughout the English-speaking world, in response to telegrams asking for comment, paid tribute to him in varying terms. All this fanfare would undoubtedly have embarrassed Atkinson, in his lifetime a shy and retiring man whose name rarely appeared in the *Star* outside its masthead.

Comments appearing in other Canadian newspapers inclined to be sparing of praise. The *Financial Post* admitted "the sincerity of his zeal for social reform, his interest in the underprivileged, and his humanitarian concern for minorities," but declared that "seldom did he credit other successful business men with motives as high as his own." Rather he tried "to build up in the public mind the idea that big business and malefaction are synonymous."

"He counted his success less in direct influence upon public opinion than in the material factors underlying newspaper publishing," said the Toronto *Globe and Mail*.

But the Montreal *Star* called him a "genius," the Kingston *Whig-Standard* a "warmly human man of great spirit and brilliant mind," and the Ottawa *Journal* declared that "he did not build his newspaper and his wealth for the sake of power or prestige." The Vancouver *Sun* said, that "paradoxically the wealthy *Star* was one of the most powerful and consistent champions of the 'little man' in our times."

Writing in her weekly paper, *News*, Miss Judith Robinson said:

A large daily newspaper produced at a profit is not necessarily corrupt, even though that paper has given much space to the condemnation of the profit motive in business. But the publisher who regards news as a product to be prepared, packaged and sold for profit, like any other product, is apt to be corrupt. For news is not lard or sausage meat.

At his funeral service, I heard the Rev. Dr. Peter Bryce describe Atkinson as "a great Christian" who had been the champion of all that was noble and good, a genuine friend to labour, and a philanthropist keenly interested in life's unfortunates.

Dr. Bryce had had many contacts with Atkinson. All these showed him the finest qualities of his newspaper friend. The *Star* had aided him in carrying out many charitable enterprises. Their friendship dated back to the days when British immigrants were pouring into the Earlscourt district of Toronto, and Dr. Bryce was a young man working among them. Atkinson gave him space to speak for the newcomers. Later Bryce wrote articles on social problems for the *Star*. He had good reason to think well of the publisher.

But business men condemned Atkinson for his attacks on their ethics and practices. They questioned his sincerity as a champion of labour, and charged him with inciting unrest and strikes to sell his papers. He was, they said, a fellow business man who sold them down the river for profit, a traitor to his own class.

The late Acton Burrows, Toronto publisher of trade journals, once said that "no man in Canada knows the cash value of a conviction better than J. E. Atkinson." His enemies called him "Holy Joe." The nickname was given him, wrote B. K. Sandwell in *Saturday Night,*

for much the same reason as that which led a great British Conservative to say of Gladstone that he did not mind so much his pulling an ace out of his sleeve, but he did hate to hear him say that God had put it there. Mr. Atkinson was always pulling aces out of his sleeve. That is not against the rules in either of those games. Mr. Atkinson was, however, completely convinced not only that God had put them there, but that he was using them as God intended they should be used.

The *Star's* publisher was no more a great saint than many other men who make millions. Neither, on the other hand, was he wicked, nor as hypocritical as he was often painted.

Some of us were so close to Atkinson that it was easier to see his virtues than his faults. The better you know a man the less likely you are to be over-critical. Twenty years have passed since I was closely associated with him, and I am still grateful for his kindness, his interest, his appreciation and the opportunity he gave me, though at the end I was bitterly disappointed. His character remains for me something of an enigma.

Certainly there were inconsistencies between Atkinson the social crusader, and Atkinson the keen business man. Although greatly interested in the welfare of mankind as a whole, that interest did not always extend to individual men. On occasion he could be exceedingly kind to some, while shutting his eyes to cruelties done to others in the *Star's* name, and often as a result of his orders.

In the early days especially, it was necessary to watch every penny, and to demand close budgeting and efficiency in each department. Atkinson kept close touch with everything that was going on, and made himself master of every phase of newspaper publishing. He was not only a business man, with an intimate knowledge of advertising and circulation techniques, but he had the respect of all the mechanics because he could talk to them in their own language about their machines, and would often suggest new ways of solving problems.

There was an informal and cordial relationship between the Chief and his staff. His office was on the same floor as the editorial rooms, and he would often drop in for a chat with editors and reporters. He expected hard work, of course, from everyone. But we looked upon ourselves as the *Star* family, with Atkinson as our kindly father. Though salaries were not large, even for key men, there was security of employment, and if anyone fell ill, pay went on just the same. In cases of need, the *Star* even paid doctors' and hospital bills.

But as time went on, and especially when the Chief's son-in-law, H. C. Hindmarsh, became managing editor, the family idea vanished. A newly-hired reporter asked Hindmarsh how long he had to work for the paper before he could consider himself a member of the *Star* family. "There is no *Star* family," was the gruff reply.

There was no longer any security of editorial employment. The staff turnover became the largest of any Canadian newspaper, and it was a standing joke in the fraternity that to be fired from the *Star* was a guarantee of success elsewhere. Men who had worked for the *Star* for the greater part of their business lives found themselves on the outside either by their own or official choice.

Like most other employers, Atkinson expected his heads of departments to take personal responsibility for his unpleasant decisions. The habit was catching. Sometimes the managing editor would look to his subordinates to pass on orders for dismissal or salary cuts, even though these were in conflict with their own judgment.

In his presidential office, Atkinson would observe that expenses were cutting too heavily into earnings. Off would go a note to Bone or Hindmarsh to cut ten, twenty or thirty per cent in costs. Slashing expenses was easier in the editorial department than in any other. It is less concerned with bringing in actual cash than the advertising and circulation departments. If editors and reporters are reduced in number, those who remain can always work harder.

More than once an "economy wave" struck the editorial department just before Christmas. When, on one of these occasions, Hindmarsh dropped thirteen reporters from the payroll, he doubtless did not deserve the opprobrium which came his way. He was only carrying out orders from higher up.

Though as time went on Atkinson paid good salaries to those who had helped him build the *Star,* he did not carry any of them along with him to even modest wealth through stock ownership.

I once approached Atkinson with the proposal that I invest some of my savings in the *Star.* I was told there was no stock for sale. It was his ambition to own every share, and, in the end, he all but succeeded. That, of course, was his right. Generous bonuses were paid to key men at the year's end, but many would have preferred ownership of shares in the enterprise they were helping to build.

When the sales tax was imposed upon newsprint used in daily papers, magazines were exempted to enable them to meet American competition. Atkinson shrewdly turned this to his profit. The *Star Weekly* had always been sold with a Saturday news section, and classed as a newspaper. Atkinson dropped the news section, which had become a bit of a nuisance anyway, and claimed tax exemption on the *Weekly* as a magazine. Ottawa ruled in his favour, saving him many thousands of dollars yearly.

It did not pay to cross Atkinson. At the opening of Maple Leaf Gardens, the building manager was annoyed to see ragged newsboys with *Stars* and *Telegrams* under their arms pushing their way through the crowds of customers. He ordered them off the premises. Atkinson persuaded C. O. Knowles of the *Telegram* to join him in making a major issue of it. The Gardens Company was notified of a substantial increase in advertising rates. It retaliated by using smaller space, but in the long run the newspapers were the gainers and shared in this way in the success of professional hockey. In view of the large amount of free publicity given to sports Atkinson considered this a fair way of securing a part of the profits.

The *Star* did not always come off best in a clash, however. In the early days of the rotogravure section of the *Weekly,* Hindmarsh sent Claude Pascoe up to Eaton's art gallery to secure some colour prints for the front page. Hindmarsh selected a few and used them. They were for the most part very cheap and inferior reproductions.

A few weeks later an excited and redfaced Englishman came into my office and asked who was responsible for the use of pictures on which he held the copyright. He wanted to collect damages. I took him to Hindmarsh, who offered to make a modest settlement. The Englishman, however, wanted more, and was prepared to go to court, and of course he had the law on his side. I do not know what was finally paid, but I know the *Star* had to pay handsomely for violating the copyright on those pictures.

Again when McMaster University, then located on Bloor Street in Toronto, was considering the acceptance of a site from a group of Hamilton citizens, a series of interviews with an "eminent legal authority" appeared in the *Star.* It was stated that the terms of the late Senator McMaster's will would not permit the removal of the university from Toronto. The "eminent legal authority" turned out to be Chief Justice Sir William Mulock, who was a part owner of a tract of land at the head of Avenue Road, on the outskirts of Toronto, on which McMaster had secured an option before the Hamilton offer developed. Sir William was also a shareholder in the *Star.* But this attempt to hold McMaster in Toronto failed.

When it came to dealings with trade unions, Atkinson was a shrewd negotiator. He knew all the ropes, and could meet union leaders on their own ground. Toronto's other publishers recognized his ability in this respect, and again and again he was asked to negotiate contracts with unions on their behalf. Generally he drove hard bargains, much harder than the unions expected from one who had championed the cause of labour in his paper.

It is hard to reconcile the *Star's* reputation as the advocate of union labour with its measures to thwart the attempt of its special writers and reporters to form a unit of the Toronto Newspaper Guild affiliated with the C.I.O. This fight took place in 1941, while Atkinson was living. The story, as told by former employees who were casualties, is one that rivals other famous conflicts between capital and labour.

Bill Law, former *Star Weekly* artist, told me that when the unit was being organized, it became clear that management was sternly opposed. Staff members were interviewed singly, and advised not to join. Many were persuaded to resign from the Guild. Atkinson took the position that unless Guild units were organized on the other Toronto papers, there could be none on the *Star*, and the other papers had turned thumbs down. The attempt to organize a *Star* unit collapsed and from then on, Law says, the leaders in the movement were marked men. They were relieved of their jobs at the slightest pretext. A *Star* executive, he added, showed me a list of names, all marked off, and boasted that they had now all been fired, the last one for allegedly taking time off to write for a local magazine. A few days later this "last one" blew his brains out.

The fight was renewed after Atkinson's death, and the Guild now has gained recognition at the *Star*.

I believe that there were in reality two J. E. Atkinsons. The first was a young, ambitious, hard-working, thrifty and shrewd idealist. He believed what he preached on his editorial pages and endeavoured to practise it, while building up the *Star* under conditions which demanded a close watch on expenditures. He endeavoured to be fair to his employees.

Mrs. Atkinson, a charming and friendly woman, did much at that time to help in establishing happy relationships among the staff. When asked by a friend about the origin of his interest in social well-being, Atkinson replied: "The Christian religion, of course, and my wife. I found she was away in advance of me in her realization of the importance of social services and also of the obligation of the state to its people."

The second J. E. Atkinson was a product of the *Star* skyscraper. He created it and it possessed him. It became his master, a Frankenstein monster which demanded of him that he make the *Star* and his bank balance ever bigger.

The building of the skyscraper was a triumph of Atkinson thrift. Sufficient profits had been made at the old offices to make possible the building of the $5,000,000, twenty-one-storey structure without borrowing a single dollar. It was a financial sensation in Toronto.

Mrs. Atkinson died in 1931, two years after the new building was occupied. With her companionship and the support of her idealism gone, the Chief gave his whole attention to amassing a great fortune. And he had the Midas touch. *Star* and *Star Weekly* cash registers rang merrily, until it was said that the business was earning more than a million dollars a year before taxes.

Atkinson drew more and more into himself. He belonged to the National Club, but he was lonely there. Few of its members did more than nod to him. Perhaps he feared the formation of close friendships might prove embarrassing to him as publisher of the *Star*.

But while he had few intimate friends in Toronto, he was in the close confidence of both Sir Wilfrid Laurier and W. L. Mackenzie King. To break with Laurier over the formation of a National Government during the First World War was a bitter experience. His friendship with W. L. Mackenzie King suffered no such break and they had a firm faith in each other to the end. Mr. King was a frequent visitor at the Atkinson home in Toronto, and Atkinson paid many visits to Ottawa to talk over national problems with his friend at Laurier House.

In King's private file of newspaper clippings was a large folder devoted to Atkinson, and his tribute at the time of the latter's death revealed interesting details of their early association. Said the Canadian Prime Minister:

Our friendship began when he was a young reporter and came to Berlin (now Kitchener) to report the criminal assizes. I was then a student in the High School. He visited our home "Woodside," and the friendship he then formed with members of our family continued through the years.

For a short time during the election of 1896, when I was a reporter on the staff of the Toronto *Evening Globe*, I shared Mr. Atkinson's desk. He was then on the staff of the morning paper. When he subsequently became publisher of the Toronto *Star*, and when I was pursuing studies abroad, he bought and paid for articles from me. During my public life, Mr. Atkinson was as unfailing in his support of me as leader of the Liberal party as he was constant in his personal friendship.

In his new skyscraper, the Chief's grey-walled office was much farther from editorial, business, advertising and mechanical departments than in the old building. His deafness troubled him increasingly, and, even with a hearing aid, it was often difficult for him to carry on a conversation. For days on end he saw only his chief executives who came at his call. Loss of daily contact with his staff made him a lonely man in his own household. His earlier hobbies of driving high powered cars and speeding his motorboat through the Muskoka Lakes were of little consolation in the later years.

Atkinson's private benefactions were many, and he helped a large number of worthy causes. He provided considerable sums for research in various Toronto hospitals. In earlier days he had given his time as a member of the board of St. John's Convalescent Home, and a director of Grace Hospital. Few will ever know the extent of his generosity, because most of his gifts were made anonymously.

In his later years he could have given himself wholeheartedly to philanthropy, while the *Star* carried on. He could have put the Atkinson Charitable Foundation into operation in his lifetime and himself got some of the fun of distributing *Star* profits. For some reason, he could not let go. He worked to the finish, hanging on to his power and adding daily to his wealth.

Despite his early religious training, Atkinson was not, in his later years, an active churchman. Although a member of Timothy Eaton Memorial Church, he was not often in his pew. His failing hearing may have had much to do with this. It was rumoured that he had made a gift of $100,000 to a United Church cause, but it was later revealed that the amount was smaller. His giving was done for the most part privately, through his own Church.

As a young man he had thought of entering the Christian ministry, but some of the dogma insisted on in those days repelled him. He had worked out his own interpretation of Christ's teachings, based on his own reading of the Bible. He regarded them essentially as a social rather than a theological gospel.

It is said that as age crept up on him he became an agnostic. If so, the story of his last hours, told by Pierre Berton in *Maclean's Magazine,* would seem to indicate a return to his early faith.

On May 7, 1948, in the dark of the night, the sick old man struggled up from his bed. His two nurses tried to subdue him. "Let me alone!" he cried out in a cracked voice. "Let me alone! I want to get down on my knees and pray." These were almost his last words. Next day he died.

# 39 ⋘

## *I Leave the "Star"*

ALTHOUGH I RESENTED IT bitterly at the time, I have reason to thank Harry Hindmarsh for forcing my resignation from the *Star Weekly* in February, 1933.

His action opened a door through which I passed into a much happier life than I had ever led in my twenty-one years of editorship —even in the days before Hindmarsh succeeded John R. Bone as his father-in-law's right hand man.

It was Bone who put me in charge of the *Star Weekly,* and for seventeen years I had his confidence. I was free to steer the ship in my own way, under his general direction and that of President Atkinson on matters of policy.

Hindmarsh joined the *Star* shortly after I took over the editorship of the *Weekly.* During the early years, when I had no writing staff of my own but depended on outside contributors, we got along well. But when, at the end of the First World War, I gradually added such writers as Gregory Clark, Frederick Griffin, Charles Vining, R. C. Reade and others to my staff, friction developed. Repeatedly, and generally without notice, Hindmarsh would draft these men to cover major news stories for the *Daily Star.* Frequently I arrived at the office to find that I had no writers with whom to produce a magazine section.

The *Daily* was paying the *Weekly's* deficits in those early years, so it was fair that we should help out. But I had to have some assurance that I would not be constantly denuded of my staff.

I protested to Bone, and he ordered that no *Weekly* staff men were to be drafted without his approval. This did not please Hindmarsh. When Bone died, and Hindmarsh became managing editor, my writers were again drafted without notice. I appealed to Atkinson, who ruled that the *Weekly* should receive more consideration.

One Thursday I sent Fred Griffin out of town to get a front page article. On Monday, when his copy should have been in, I saw in the *Daily* a feature story of a big storm on Lake Superior under Griffin's by-line. I realized my assignment had not been covered.

When Griffin came in, I remarked mildly that I wished he had let me know. Fagged after a sleepless forty-eight hours, Griffin blew up, and reported to Hindmarsh, who sent for me and berated me for "bawling out" Griffin, which I had not done. "If I had been Mr. Griffin, I would have smashed your face for you," he roared. Next day Fred Griffin apologized for having lost his temper, and later wrote me a most affectionate letter.

For two or three years after Bone's death, however, things went fairly smoothly. Hindmarsh was busy changing the *Daily Star* into the kind of paper he thought it should be. But at last the day came when he felt he must also change the *Star Weekly*. It needed, he thought, more zip and boom and hurrah, and should follow more closely the highly successful pattern of Hearst's *American Weekly*. Besides, it could be produced more cheaply by using more syndicate material.

My editorial policy through the years had been to publish a distinctively Canadian magazine. Hindmarsh, of course, as managing editor, responsible only to J. E. Atkinson, had the right to put his ideas into effect. I did not know to what extent the Chief was in accord with those ideas, having no direct word from him, but I naturally struggled to maintain the Canadian characteristics which up to that time had had Atkinson's approval and backing.

One June morning, in 1932, Hindmarsh asked me to let him see all manuscripts I had accepted for use in the *Star Weekly*. I gathered them up, more than forty in all, and gave them to him. Three days later they came back with a note stating that most of them were no good and should be returned to the writers. I walked into Hindmarsh's office and protested.

"I am not questioning your judgment," I said. "But I have accepted these manuscripts in the name of the *Star Weekly* and have promised they will be paid for."

"That makes no difference. Send them back. They are no good." Hindmarsh's face was crimson.

"But we promised to pay," I protested.

"Send them back. We will not pay for them."

"If the *Star* will not pay for them, then I will," I declared. "My name is signed to those letters of acceptance, and I feel morally bound to protect my name."

Realizing I meant it, Hindmarsh cooled down. I suggested we return the manuscripts with one-third the amount we would have paid on publication, explaining there had been a change of policy and giving the writer full permission to sell them elsewhere. Hindmarsh agreed and I returned the manuscripts with about $800 in cash, and wiped the slate clean.

This incident had an amusing sequel. Some eighteen months after I left the *Star*, my successor wired to a Maritime writer, whose work had been popular with *Star Weekly* readers in my day, asking him to send in some stories. He complied. Hindmarsh approved them, and they were published. But when the bookkeeper was writing cheques, he noticed that once before a story bearing a similar title had been paid for by the *Star*. He informed Hindmarsh, and a wire was sent the writer charging him with obtaining money by false pretenses by selling the same story twice to the *Star Weekly*.

Back came the answer that the story (one of those which Hindmarsh had rejected in my day as unsuitable) had been returned after acceptance and paid for in part, but with full permission to sell it where he pleased. If the *Star* wished to accept it a second time, that suited him perfectly. After some dispute, the cheque was forwarded for the full amount.

Finally, Hindmarsh decided to take over the *Star Weekly* and turn me into a rubber stamp. If I wanted to buy anything, I must submit it for his approval. He next ordered that all manuscripts should be read by other members of the staff. If Clark and Griffin supported my judgment, it would go to him for final O.K. My stature was steadily shrinking. One more prima donna was being deflated.

During my twenty-one years of editorship, the *Weekly* circulation had grown from 16,000 to a peak of 250,000, and without extensive promotion campaigns. The paper was making profits of half a million dollars a year.

In November, 1932, Hindmarsh informed me that it had been decided to bring in Main Johnson as editor of the *Weekly*, and that I would become associate editor with my salary cut by one-third.

Atkinson asked to see me. He greeted me kindly and hoped the new arrangement would be a happier one for me. Praising my work throughout the years, he expressed regret that "Harry" and I had not pulled well together. Henceforth there would be no necessity of friction as Johnson would be directly responsible to Hindmarsh.

I thanked him for the kind words which made the pill less bitter. Though the cut in salary was a little hard to swallow, I felt that I would now be relieved of a lot of worry and would be settled in a more comfortable position for the rest of my working days.

At first I did not want any public announcement of the change. On second thought, I decided it would be better to get all the favourable publicity I could, and pledge the *Star* to an open acknowledgment of my new position. In a note to me Atkinson said, "I think you take the correct view."

On December 1, 1932, The *Star* printed on its front page an article by Gregory Clark three-quarters of a column in length, together with a photograph of myself. The two-column heading read "Sees *Star Weekly* Triumph of Great Newspaper Ideals: J. H. Cranston Hands Over Active Editorship After 21 Years' Command."

It announced that I was to be associate editor and said:

Throughout its development from the least to the greatest of Canadian publications Mr. Cranston has not been merely the faithful interpreter of the policy of the publishers, but has infused his own personality, restraint and sensitiveness into a journal which, while appealing to all classes, as its very substantial circulation shows, may still enter the most strictly critical and old-fashioned home to be found in the remote villages of the country.

It paid tribute to my "great success achieved in promoting the development of native Canadian writers," and told the story of the successful rivalry with the *Sunday World* and the latter's final absorption.

It ended with words which seemed to me, after twenty-nine years spent in the *Star's* service, to constitute a definite promise:

As associate editor, Mr. Cranston will continue to give The *Star Weekly* the benefit of his long experience in gauging popular interests.

Nevertheless, just eight weeks later, after I had worked night and day helping my successor to become acquainted with his new task, Hindmarsh informed me I was to be removed from the staff of the *Star Weekly* altogether.

I was given two options. I could accept reduction to the ranks— that is, a job handling copy on the *Daily Star*—with another cut of fifty per cent in salary; or I could resign. If I resigned, I would be paid a year's salary.

In amazement I demanded the reason for action which went counter to everything I had been promised.

"Mr. Johnson tells me he is not satisfied with the fiction the *Star Weekly* has been printing," replied Hindmarsh.

"Why, only yesterday Mr. Johnson told me how pleased he was with the co-operation he was receiving from me," I said.

"Well," said Hindmarsh, "I had to drag it out of him."

I did not point out that all the fiction the *Star Weekly* had been printing for months past had been approved by Hindmarsh himself. I had continued to select for Johnson the kind of stories Hindmarsh liked.

Hindmarsh also declared I had defied orders the previous day by asking one of the artists how soon a certain illustration would be ready, when I had been told the art department was no longer under my jurisdiction. As a matter of fact, I had done this to help the new editor, who was finding things a bit difficult. The foreman of the engraving department, who had charge of the artists, had reported this breach of the rules to Hindmarsh, and sat there smiling while I was being reprimanded.

I resigned immediately by letter—not to Hindmarsh, but to J. E. Atkinson, who had first hired me in 1904. I expressed surprise that the promise made to me in private by himself, and publicly in the *Star,* had been so quickly and lightly broken. I told him how shocked I was to be forced to leave the *Star* in this fashion. But I did not stress the bitterness I felt in being offered such a humiliating alternative.

The next day I received a letter from him at my home. It read:

Dear Mr. Cranston:

I need not say with what extreme regret I see you leaving The *Star.* You have always had my generous good will, and I am sorry that relationships upstairs have resulted in your resignation. The leaving bonus of a year's salary is with the idea of recognizing your long connection with the paper and my appreciation of your past services. I suppose you intended in submitting your resignation that it should take effect immediately, and I am giving instructions that a cheque be issued to you at once. The yearly bonus is treated as part of your salary.

Believe me,

Yours very sincerely,<br>J. E. Atkinson.

From my letter of acknowledgment I give a couple of sentences:

I am happy in the knowledge that I leave the organization with a proud record of achievement, with the good will of all who have worked under me, and with no blot on my character. I thank you most sincerely for the opportunity you gave me as editor of The *Star Weekly,* and if I take more credit than is my due for its phenomenal growth in circulation and influence perhaps I may be forgiven.

Throughout the years, my personal relations with Atkinson had always been pleasant. He was uniformly kind and thoughtful. My salary was advanced from time to time without request from me. For years I was allowed three weeks' holidays, a privilege not given to many staff members. When I was ill in hospital, he and his wife visited me. He accepted invitations to my home, and my wife and I were entertained in his. When my wife and I went to Europe on a two months' holiday, I was given leave of absence with pay. More than once he informed me that he had stood between me and the wrath of his son-in-law.

When John R. Bone died suddenly in June, 1928, I wrote Atkinson a letter expressing sympathy with him in the loss of his right hand man, who would be missed by all of us. I received from him a reply written in his own hand, expressing the genuine feeling of a man who appreciated and reciprocated the loyalty of those who had been long associated with him. It read:

My dear Cranston:

You cannot know how much your note has touched me. To those of us who belong to the older circle in the office, Mr. Bone's death will leave a vacancy never to be filled. I hope it will bring closer together those of us who are left. You must yourself take good care of health and strength. I am glad you are going to take a longer holiday this summer. You must ease off work as much as possible in the meantime.

For years he had been my ideal of a newspaper publisher, and I believed absolutely in his integrity. I could always go to his office when I felt I was suffering an injustice and be sure of a fair hearing.

The action to which he was a party shook my faith in J. E. Atkinson.

I had no further contacts with him until some time after I had moved to Midland to become the publisher of the district weekly newspaper.

I had become interested in the renovation of Calvary Baptist Church. Having been successful in getting help from a number of Toronto friends, I decided to appeal to Atkinson. Back came a cheque for $50, together with a cordial note.

In 1937 the Bowmanville *Statesman* published a story relating to Atkinson's boyhood. It asserted that he had once pumped the organ in the little Methodist Church in Newcastle. I reprinted the story, and playfully commented that this might have accounted for Atkinson's subsequent dislike of organs, which found expression in the *Star's* slogan, "A Newspaper Not An Organ." Shortly afterwards I received a letter from him in his own hand. He said that he was four years old in 1870 when he was supposed to have pumped the organ, and suggested it must have been one of his brothers.

"I am glad to have the error bring me such a nice friendly reminiscing article from you," he wrote. "I am more pleased than I can say to recognize the good will in it to me personally. You are doing wonders with the *Free Press*. More power and prosperity to you."

Possibly the deepest satisfaction I ever experienced as publisher of the Midland paper came to me on the day I showed Atkinson through my plant.

He had come to Midland on an errand of mercy, and, when I caught sight of his big car on the street, I invited him to inspect my office. I wanted him to see how well I was established after my unhappy farewell to the *Star*. He was publisher of the *Star* and the *Star Weekly*, worth twenty millions or more. Both of these papers I had helped to build. Now I owned a weekly newspaper, worth little more than as many thousands. But I could talk to him as one publisher to another.

My invitation was accepted and together we went over the premises. Atkinson congratulated me and wished me continued success.

When I sold the *Free Press Herald* to my son, I thought it would be a good opportunity to obtain further light on the anomalous character of my former chief. I wrote Atkinson, recalling that I had been editor of the *Star Weekly* through its difficult years and into its era of greatest expansion and circulation. I enquired whether, now I was retired, and in view of my twenty-nine years of service, the *Star* would consider paying me a small pension.

His reply seemed to me characteristic. He could not fall in with my idea. But if my son Bill, who had just bought the paper from me, would like to join the editorial staff of the *Daily Star,* Hindmarsh would be glad to hire him at a stipulated salary. This would have meant, of course, that I would have to buy back the paper and return to work.

I had a rather wicked pleasure in thanking him for his offer. I told him I doubted that Bill would be interested, since he had refused two offers, each involving more than twice the proffered *Star* salary, to come back to our own publishing business.

That was our last exchange of correspondence.

# 40 ⫷

## *Search for New Fields*

WHEN THE NEWS of my resignation got around the *Star Weekly* office, Jimmy Frise came to me and said: "Boss, if you can get another Sunday paper started in Toronto, I will go with you. I think most of the other boys would too." Greg Clark also intimated something of the sort.

I appreciated these generous offers of help, but I had no plans. Moreover I did not want anyone on the *Weekly* staff to get into trouble by offering to go with me to another paper.

After twenty-nine straight years of nervously exhausting work, I determined to take a long rest before seeking a new connection.

But I found it difficult to holiday. I wanted some assurance of a new post, and naturally preferred one similar to that I had left. But there was none available. So I tried to create one.

I drew up a prospectus for a five-cent weekly paper that would be produced more cheaply than the *Star Weekly,* but would carry many of the features that had made it popular, and stories and articles by Canadian writers who were my personal friends. I presented it to the Toronto *Evening Telegram.* They considered it for six months before I received a negative reply. I tried in four or five other quarters but received no encouragement. I am glad these overtures failed. It would have been a hard and unpleasant fight against the *Star.*

The depression was having its effect on Canadian newspapers. All, except perhaps the *Star,* were having financial difficulties. Salaries were being cut, and men who held their jobs counted themselves lucky.

I determined to realize a long-cherished ambition to own a town weekly newspaper. But about this time I was invited by W. G. Jaffray of the *Globe* to reorganize the *Globe's* library which, he said, was in a deplorable condition. I accepted, with the proviso that I might remain free to pursue my negotiations for a weekly newspaper.

Jaffray, a fundamentalist Presbyterian with a keen interest in foreign missions, was regarded as a crank because he refused to allow cigarette advertising in the *Globe*. He had an intense dislike for J. E. Atkinson, whom he considered a menace to journalism in Canada. But he was very friendly to me, especially after he learned I was a deacon in Yorkminster Baptist Church.

One day Jaffray surprised me by saying he thought the *Globe* and the *Mail and Empire* would have to unite if either was to survive. He suggested that I approach John Scott, publisher of the *Mail and Empire,* and sound him out on the possible sale of his paper. Scott told me he would be glad to hear what Jaffray had in mind, but he doubted whether he had any intention of buying the *Mail and Empire.* It was not many years later that George McCullagh, backed by William Wright, bought both papers, and merged them in the present *Globe and Mail.*

When the library renovation job was finished, Jaffray suggested that I might like to write editorials for the *Globe*. But I knew the paper was having a hard struggle to survive, and that salaries were low. Besides, I had set my heart on acquiring a newspaper of my own.

Meanwhile, between intervals of working in the *Globe* library, I took on two jobs of widely different character. One was for Hugh Eayrs, president of The Macmillan Company of Canada whose first literary work I had published in the *Star Weekly* when he came from England. He invited me to revise and bring up to date the volume on Canada in the "Peeps at Many Lands" series published by Black's of London. I found it necessary to entirely re-write the book, and my first literary endeavour to go between stiff covers proved an interesting venture.

The other job was the editorship of a tabloid weekly, *The Straight Furrow,* published by the Conservative party in the interests of the Henry Government in Ontario. This was a seven to ten weeks pre-election job, offered me by C. Lesslie Wilson, publisher of a string of free distribution papers, on whose presses the *Furrow* was to be printed. I stipulated that I should be responsible only for the general make-up of the paper—non-political features and pictures, layouts, copy-handling, headings, and so on—and not for editorials and other propaganda material.

R. Home Smith, one of the Conservative strategists, angrily protested this appointment of a "damned Grit" who had worked for
"Holy Joe" Atkinson. But when Wilson explained the circumstances
of my leaving the *Star*, he made no further objection.

Unfortunately, the Conservative strategy was ill-conceived. The
Henry Government was suffering from old age. Its strategists thought
they could defeat the young, vigorous, and ebullient "Mitch" Hepburn
by lampooning him as a brash and half-baked rustic. I warned them
that ridicule was a dangerous weapon, but Home Smith had his way.

Hepburn's face lent itself well to caricature, and the artists made
the most of it. When his car killed a cow on the highway, a cartoon
pictured him as saying, "For years I have shot the bull; now I have
killed a cow." Another showed him as a circus clown, supplementing
the shortage of comedians on the radio. When he said he "swung
well to the left" in his views, he was represented as a Red.

Frank Mann ("Six Bit") Harris wrote a clever series of full-page
articles portraying "Mitch" as a roughneck. In one he was likened to
a bootlegger who fooled his patrons at the ball park by pouring beer
into mugs with false bottoms and blowing up rich foam with an air
pump.

A good job was done in character sketches of the various cabinet
ministers with portraits by the rising young Toronto artist, Grant
Macdonald. But when a photograph was taken of Premier George
Henry on his farm at Oriole, on which he had done little manual
labour for many years, he was posed in a brand new pair of overalls.
The stiff creases were still in them and they looked fresh out of a
mail order catalogue—as well they may have been. Ontario's dirt
farmers were quick to note those creases and Liberal orators found in
them a new source of political ammunition.

The Tory attempt to laugh the Liberal leader off the map was a
mistake. Old Man Ontario resented the refusal of the Conservatives
to take Hepburn's criticisms of the government seriously, and to
answer them in detail. The ridicule backfired.

Thus, while I had nothing to do with this strategy, and wrote
none of the propaganda, I am afraid I had a part in making Mitch
Hepburn premier of Ontario.

Finding a weekly paper that was for sale was proving a harder
task than I had imagined. Despite the depression, owners wanted
to hang on.

The *Age-Dispatch* of Strathroy, Ontario, nearly came into my hands. One of the brothers who owned it, Evans by name, wanted to sell; the other did not. The day before the deal was to be closed, negotiations, conducted for me by J. F. Mackay, were broken off.

In the case of the Tillsonburg *News*, one partner, Aldridge, wanted to sell and retire; but the other partner, H. F. Johnston, decided to buy him out.

Some months were spent in fruitless negotiations to buy the daily Port Hope *Guide*. I went to Kirkland Lake to look over the *News*. It was a fine plant, but I did not feel enough of a pioneer at 54 to settle in that northern clime.

Finally I heard that the Midland *Free Press* could be bought.

Friends warned me that the town was bankrupt and fully one-third of its people were on relief. They said it was a burnt out lumber town that had shot its bolt. One day in Toronto, I talked with Douglas L. White Jr., who had been one of Midland's "big four" industrialists in its palmy days. What did he think of the town's future?

"My boy," he said, "I have seen Midland in far worse condition than it is today, and I have seen it climb back to prosperity. I believe it will do so again. If I were a young man I would ask no better opportunity."

I also consulted A. J. B. Gray, then attached to the Ontario Government's Department of Municipal Affairs, who was supervising Midland's finances. Though not as optimistic as White, he thought Midland had a real chance of recovery, and that possibly I could help.

As my wife and I drove through the lovely countryside that circles south-eastern Georgian Bay to visit Midland for the first time, we were charmed by the town's setting. Midland, we found, was a place of comfortable looking homes, well-kept lawns and gardens, and paved roads. The main street was wide and clean, bordered by good stores and houses. The big Midland-Simcoe grain elevator, gleaming white against the blue of the bay, was impressive.

A town that looked so good could not be all bad. I said to my wife, "This is our town!" It was love at first sight.

We found Alfred S. Wilkes, publisher, editor and chief shareholder of the *Free Press* ready to sell. He confessed that he had lost faith in the town's future. Besides, he was in poor health and wanted to retire. He held fifty-two per cent. of the stock. The rest was owned by Midland businessmen. I wanted all or nothing. This time I was going to be my own master. Finally, terms of purchase were arranged. On June 1, 1935, I took over the *Free Press,* and my wife, our son William (who had just graduated from McMaster University), and our younger boy Tom, became residents of Midland.

At last I had realized a life-long dream. I was to publish my own paper. Yet it was not mine alone. Though they held no stock, the people of Midland, Penetanguishene, and the surrounding towns and farms of North Simcoe were vitally concerned in its future. It must serve their interests worthily. I was conscious that we had become custodians of a public trust.

# 41 ≪≪

## On and Off the Record

BUT DESPITE OUR MOVE from the provincial metropolis to a town of
but 7,000 people, not all my newspapering in the succeeding years was
confined to Midland. Indeed the high peak of all my journalistic
adventures was an interview with Winston Churchill at Ottawa on
December 30, 1941. Of course there were nearly fifty other newspapermen there, but, for me, there seemed but two persons present.

The British Prime Minister had just addressed a combined
meeting of the Canadian Senate and House in the Commons chamber.
Everyone who heard his address that day, whether within Parliament
or by radio, will never forget one phrase. Mr. Churchill told how,
just before the fall of France, he sought to encourage the French
government to continue their fight against Hitler's hordes. "I warned
them that Britain would fight on alone whatever they did, but the
French generals told their premier and his divided cabinet that in
three weeks England would have her neck wrung like a chicken."

He paused, looked up from his manuscript, chuckled and exclaimed, "Some chicken! Some neck!" and all the English-speaking
world roared.

At the conclusion of his address, a number of Canadian newspapermen were admitted to the Liberal caucus room back of the
Commons for a face to face talk with Churchill. Everything was to
be "off the record," but so many years have elapsed and the war is
so long over, there is no longer need for secrecy.

My chair in the second row was a fortunate choice. Churchill sat
just opposite me and less than ten feet away. I could study his face
at close range and watch the play of his emotions.

179

The British leader drew from his pocket one of his famous long black cigars; then fumbled for a match. He had none. Prime Minister King, a non-smoker, put on a mock show of hunting for one. However, pipe smoker R. B. Hanson, then Conservative house leader, quickly produced a lucifer and Churchill was happy.

To break the ice, King asked his guest if he cared to comment on the Canadian government's recognition of the Vichy regime, a policy which had been hotly criticized. Churchill replied that it was a distinct advantage to the Allies to have a window through which they could look at what was happening in France. King smiled.

Then the barrage started. Churchill trusted us absolutely, and told us many things which at that time would have made sensational newspaper copy. And to nearly every answer he gave a humorous twist.

It was fun to watch his face. Fatter than I expected, it had the high pink of a baby. His twinkling eyes all but disappeared when he laughed. He would be discussing seriously some question of high policy when, suddenly, a whimsical idea would strike and his whole body begin to quiver. Most people's smiles begin on their faces. Churchill's climbed from the hips up.

A reporter asked if there was a chance that the Italians might sue for a separate peace. Churchill began by speaking of his sincere regard for the Italian people and of their desperate situation. Then came a mischievous grin. "Much as I would like to believe such a thing possible, I am afraid the organ grinder still has his hand on the monkey's collar."

Asked whether the Turks would likely enter the war on our side, Mr. Churchill replied that "the Turks would like to be with us, but when they come out of their tents they see hanging before them the skeletons of twelve smaller nations, and they don't want to be the thirteenth. It would be unlucky. So back they go into their tents."

Two British battleships, the *Repulse* and the *Prince of Wales,* had just been sunk by the Japanese. A question was asked as to the wisdom of sending out such valuable capital ships without proper protection.

"It has always been my policy to give freedom of initiative to our naval commanders," countered the Prime Minister. "This sortie might have resulted in a tremendous victory. I never criticize men who err in moving towards the enemy."

"We hear considerable criticism of the British government for the inadequacy of Far Eastern defences and equipment," suggested another editor.

"Yes, that's true," said Churchill. "And what criticism the cabinet gets from the press is as nothing compared to what I give it when alone. So far as the East is concerned, we had to make the best use of what supplies we had, and it was more important to win in Libya than to divide our resources and lose in both East and West."

Some one asked if he would mind telling the true story of Rudolph Hess. We gasped. This was one of the war's top secrets and we expected him to sidestep. However, without any hesitation he gave us the full facts, but he clothed his story with such whimsical foolery that we thought he was spoofing. Every sentence was a gem. He sought to unfold the workings of Hess's mind, and mimicked Hitler's runaway pal with the skill of a great comedian.

Hess, he told us, alarmed by the unsatisfactory turn of events in Russia, planned to get Britain out of the war and possibly gain her as an ally against the Russians. He appointed himself a plenipotentiary with unlimited powers and decided to fly to Britain. He thought that if he could only get to the King, he could tell him that Hitler really loved and admired England and did not want to have to destroy her. The might of German war power would be unfolded, and the King, appalled by what he heard, would dismiss "that man Churchill" and the war would be over.

But how was he to get to the King? He looked through Burke's Peerage and came across the name of Lord Hamilton. Yes, he remembered him. They had met at the Olympic games. Hamilton, the book said, was "the king's steward." Steward? Oh, yes. That was the man who fed the King, the chap who would say "Would your majesty enjoy a piece of good roast beef today, or perhaps Your Royal Highness would prefer some breast of chicken or a drumstick? And will you have your tea now, or later?"

And Churchill bowed and scraped and went through all the antics of an obsequious waiter who was trying to interest the King in the food the royal kitchen had to offer. We howled with laughter. Then, when the King had eaten his full and was feeling happy, Hamilton would offer him a smoke and whisper in his ear about the arrival in Scotland of one of Hitler's chief aides, who had come with an offer of peace and good will.

The King would listen eagerly and excitedly, and would say, "Bring in this man Hess, and let me hear what he has to say." Then

Hess would step out from behind the window curtains where he had been hiding, and bow low to His Majesty and appeal for peace. Then the King would say, "But what will I do with this fellow Churchill? He wants to fight on until he beats you."

Then Hess would say, "Dismiss him from office, Your Majesty. Put him in jail, the war will be over, and everyone will be happy. And the British will be friends again with the Germans who admire and love them so much."

When we stopped laughing, Churchill told us how Hess had sneaked out to an airport, climbed into a plane, turned on the ignition, started the engine, speeded down the runway and was off for England before anyone knew what he was up to. Then came his landing on the estate of Lord Hamilton, his arrest and imprisonment.

I determined to ask one question just for the fun of having done it. But, when I came to speak, it was with feeling akin to stage fright.

"Mr. Churchill," I asked, "what do you consider the significance of Hitler's having dismissed General Von Keitel, and taken over supreme control of the German armies in Russia himself?"

"I am not in Hitler's confidence," the Prime Minister replied with a grin, "so I cannot say for sure. But my opinion is that it happened because of a conflict of will power between Hitler and his general. And you know," he added with a chuckle, "that boy Hitler has a hell of a will power."

Mine was the last question. Time was up, and the two Prime Ministers and the Leader of the Opposition left the room.

# 42 ⧏⧏⧏

## A Dream Comes True

TEN YEARS AFTER we arrived in Midland, my wife and I were guests of honour at a banquet under the auspices of the Midland Kiwanis Club.

The occasion was the award to the *Free Press Herald* and its publisher of the David Williams Memorial Trophy. This goes each year to the Canadian weekly newspaper adjudged to have the best editorial page.

The presentation was made by Hugh Templin, then president of the Canadian Weekly Newspapers Association and publisher of the Fergus *News-Record*. Editor Templin said he had once advised me against coming to Midland because it was "a dead town." "But," he added, "all that is changed, and a measure of the credit for the change is due to the progressive activity of the *Free Press Herald* under Mr. Cranston's direction."

Gregory Clark told stories of the days when we were colleagues on the *Star Weekly*, and Jimmy Frise of "Birdseye Centre" fame drew some of his amusing cartoons. Representatives of the Midland and Penetanguishene councils paid tributes to the *Free Press Herald*, and I was presented with a photographic exposure meter, a recognition of my life-long hobby.

It was the climax of my newspaper career, and my happiest moment. And I said so. I added that it was a great satisfaction to win the trophy, but a far greater one to have won the confidence and good will of one's fellow citizens.

It would take another book to tell the full story of my twelve happy years as publisher of the *Free Press Herald*.

At the outset it was arranged that my son Bill would take charge of the business management and the job printing, and that I would assume editorial direction. This division of duties worked admirably.

It is not a simple matter to become adjusted to a new community. Newcomers to a small town, especially if they hail from a big city, are suspect. We were not only newcomers from the city, but we had bought the town's newspaper. We had to walk carefully at first, and avoid giving the impression that we had come to make the place over. For fully six months we dodged all local issues. Constantly, however, we preached the gospel of optimism and sought to strengthen the faith of our fellow citizens in the town's ability to recover its financial equilibrium.

Before we took it over, the newspaper had been avowedly Liberal in politics. In our first issue we announced that the paper would be free in fact as well as in name. It would be tied to no party, but would give fair treatment to every shade of political opinion, without bias in either its news or comment. How well we fulfilled this promise may be judged from the fact that after one hot election the Conservative candidate told us we were the strongest supporter the Liberals had, while the Liberal candidate blamed us for the election of his Conservative rival.

As time went on, we came to be accepted by the people of the whole district as neighbours and friends. Sincerely bent on serving their interests, we supported every movement that promised to promote the welfare of the community. We backed the Ontario government in its efforts, some of them unpopular, to put the town on a sound financial footing. We did everything we could to foster the growth of industry and the tourist trade.

When we went to Midland in 1935, the district had two other papers beside the *Free Press*—the Midland *Argus*, and the Penetanguishene *Herald*. In 1936, we purchased the *Herald*, and later merged the two papers under the name of the *Free Press Herald*. In 1938 we bought and absorbed the *Argus*. The result was possibly the longest newspaper name in Canada—the *Midland-Penetanguishene Free Press Herald*.

Year after year the "F. P. H." improved its news coverage and won a consistently high rating in annual competitions. In 1941 it was awarded the Mason Trophy as the best all-round Canadian weekly newspaper, and ranked second in the editorial page judging. In succeeding years, that record was maintained. Under my son's owner-ship, the paper has won both the Mason and Williams trophies, the latter on three occasions.

Before my twelve years in the publisher's chair were up, Midland had emerged from the depression and pessimism in which we found it in 1935, and was well on the way to prosperity. Employment was at a new high. A number of new industries had been established. The shipyards, which had built many naval craft during the war, were humming with activity. Under the direction of the Ontario Depart-ment of Municipal Affairs, and the skilful management of the town treasurer, municipal finances were again on a sound basis. And the adjacent town of Penetanguishene had shown a similar record of recovery.

During the war years, my son Bill was with the Wartime Prices and Trade Board at Ottawa. When he returned, in 1946, full of energy and enthusiasm and with his experience widened by his war-time post, I felt that the time had come to turn over responsibilities of publishing to a younger man. I sold the paper to him, and confined my own activities to writing the "Sidelights" column which over the years had become a regular feature of its editorial page.

But the succeeding years were to bring me a new and stimulating kind of experience. No part of rural Ontario is richer in picturesque historic associations than my adopted land of Huronia. Here the savage Iroquois carried on their war of extermination against the Hurons, and heroic Jesuit missionaries died martyrs' deaths. Hither came Samuel de Champlain on journeys of exploration, blazing trails for the fur trade in the north. Here the pioneers of white civilization —farmers, lumbermen, fishermen, shipbuilders—thrust through the forests and over rock, and in course of time founded the ports at which fleets of grain boats poured their golden cargo into great elevators.

Archaeologists had for some time been busy near Midland, uncovering the remains of Fort Ste. Marie I, the Jesuit missionaries' "abode of peace," as well as the sites of Indian villages. Plans for the restoration of Fort Penetanguishene, outpost of the early British military forces in Ontario, were underway.

The Huronia Historic Sites and Tourist Association was doing much to draw attention to the area, already noted for the Martyrs' Shrine. When it was decided to establish in Midland a museum of Indian and pioneer life, I was elected its first president. Huronia House Museum is now internationally known as one of Ontario's leading local museums. From its inception my elder son has been its executive secretary, and an energetic worker in its interests.

I enjoyed hunting for relics of the early days in attics, sheds, barns and scrap heaps, and made many amazing discoveries. One of the most curious was a hundred-year-old pipe organ which turned up in an unused outside privy where it had been stored for safe keeping.

I became immersed in the lore of this historic area, and wrote two books—*Etienne Brûle: Immortal Scoundrel,* tracing the career of that picturesque coureur de bois who became Ontario's first white citizen, and *Huronia: Cradle of Ontario's Civilization.*

Though no longer in control of a newspaper, there were opportunities to serve my adopted town in other ways. In the fall of 1951 I initiated negotiations which led to the choice of Midland as the site for the North American factory of the German optical firm, E. Leitz of Wetzlar, one of whose world-famous Leica cameras had contributed greatly to the joy I have found in colour photography.

Now as I look back over seventy-two years, I feel that life has been very good to me. I have known the joys of struggle, adventure, and fruitful accomplishment. I have had the satisfaction of reaching the heights in two distinct fields of journalism. My family and home, my life long association with the Christian Church, the joys of travel in America and Europe, hosts of friends in many parts of the world— all these have contributed to my happiness. I have found pleasure and profit in reading and in historical research.

And to top it off, McMaster University, my alma mater, in 1949, for some mysterious reason, robed me in scarlet and conferred on me the honorary degree of Doctor of Laws.

Through the years I have worked with hundreds of interesting and worth-while people. And now in my autumn years I have the joy of living in Ontario's loveliest and most romantic county, and playing with words to keep me out of mischief.

What more could a man ask?

# L'ENVOI

There appeared in the *Free Press Herald* of December 20, 1952, the following editorial:

Editor and publisher of this newspaper for twelve years and a contributing columnist for seventeen, James Herbert Cranston died Thursday morning.

Veteran of 56 years of Canadian journalism, he was a dean among Canadian newspapermen.

J. H. Cranston believed that a newspaper should be a community servant and that its editor should lead the way in service.

In industrial and tourist promotion, in service club leadership, in historical research, in the field of Christian endeavour, he was devoted to the people of his own community and to the people of Canada.

In the written and spoken word and with his far-ranging camera, he brought inspiration to literally thousands of people.

But it was perhaps in a more personal sense that Mr. Cranston will be most missed. He believed that a newspaper had moral as well as economic responsibilities to its community. He and his newspaper stood at all times and under all circumstances for what he believed to be right in the eyes of God. He was a crusader but with no narrowness and meanness of soul. He was a friend of anyone who needed help.

Indeed to the staff of this newspaper and to his fellow journalists he will be remembered most, not for his many achievements in the publishing world, but for his unfailing understanding and kindliness. He was a man to whom personal as well as community problems could be brought in trust.

In a word, James Herbert Cranston, editor and community builder, was a good man.

To which his old friend, *Star Weekly* contributor, and minister of the years, the Rev. W. A. Cameron later added:

It is difficult to believe that Herbert Cranston is dead. Death seemed to have no part of him. He was ever full of life . . . life inspired by the love of God. That love was the greatest reality of his soul. . . . The variety of his interests, the wealth of his activities, must have had an adequate cause, and I know nothing great enough to account for them except an unfaltering realization of the divine compassion and sacrifice. . . .

As a journalist he was ever aware that our personal and national destinies depend in the long run on modes of thoughts, upon ideals, upon the gospel which is uttered from the pulpits of the press.

He knew that we have a right to look for an elevation of tone, a dignity of spirit, an earnestness of moral conviction from any publication which claims to be regarded as an organ of public opinion. In this he did not let us down.

His integrity was without a stain. He scorned the mean and hated pretence. Ostentation and show were alien to his spirit. He had a great sincerity. He could face difficult situations. He could "plod and keep the passion fresh." There was a fine blending of intellectual, moral and religious qualities in his character. . . .

He lived, prepared to die: he died, prepared to live.

— 30 —